Edinburgh Bilingual Library (4)

EDINBURGH   BILINGUAL   LIBRARY   (4)

Selected Poems

FERNANDO PESSOA

EDITED AND TRANSLATED BY
PETER RICKARD
Emmanuel College, Cambridge

UNIVERSITY   OF   TEXAS   PRESS,   AUSTIN

International Standard Book Number 0-292-72401-2
Library of Congress Catalog Card Number 71-38575
© 1971 by Peter Rickard

Printed in Great Britain by
W & J Mackay & Co Ltd, Chatham, Kent

Edinburgh Bilingual Library

FOREWORD

An imperfect knowledge of a language need be no bar to reading a work written in it if there is a good translation to help. This Library may aid those who have a wide-ranging and adventurous interest in literature to jump the hurdles of language and thus do something to help break down the barriers of specialization. That it may be helpful for courses in Comparative Literature is our hope, but not our main aim. We wish to appeal to a wider audience: first to the cultivated, serious reader of literature who is not content to remain within the English language, secondly to university students and teachers of English and of Modern Languages by inviting them to throw from outside some new light on, perhaps even discover different values in, their particular fields of specialization.

As this Bilingual Library grows it will try to map, in a necessarily limited and modest way, small areas of Western Literature through the comparison of actual texts. This it will do by building up groups of volumes to illustrate literary traditions, themes and styles. Thus no. 3, *Troubadour Lyric Poetry*, will be followed by volumes of *Minnesang*, Petrarch, Ausias March and others, which together will chart the range and significance of Courtly Love. From time to time volumes will be paired to show literary development across countries and periods. Thus, the technical and conceptual development in the reworking of classical mythology will be shown by the simultaneous publication of Poliziano's *Orfeo* and Góngora's *Polifemo*—the one at the beginning, the other at the end of The Age of Humanism.

The languages represented will be French (with Provençal), German, Italian, Portuguese, Russian, Spanish (with Catalan), and Medieval and Renaissance Latin. The translations will not be 'cribs' but good literature worth publishing in its own right. Verse will be translated into verse, except where the unfamiliarity of the language for most readers (Provençal, Catalan, Old French, Old High German) may make a more literal prose rendering advisable. In the majority of cases the Introductions will present up-to-date assessments of each author or work, or original interpretations on a scholarly level. Works already accessible in translation will only be included when we think we can offer new translations of special excellence.

A. A. Parker
GENERAL EDITOR

Contents

Fernando Pessoa

PREFACE

Relatively little of Fernando Pessoa's poetry was published in his lifetime. When he died in 1935, his work was little known, even in Portugal. He had a small following in Lisbon and in Coimbra, and was beginning to be talked about, but in no sense was he as yet a national figure. Posterity has since made handsome amends for this undeserved neglect. In Portugal and Brazil, he is today considered to be the greatest poet in the national language since Camoens. His poetry, previously unpublished, or scattered through a number of Portuguese literary journals, many of them short-lived, has been lovingly collected and published. Of his numerous prose writings, much has been published in the last few years, and the rest is being prepared for publication.

In recent years, his fame has spread to other countries. Selections from his poetry have been translated into French,[1] German,[2] Spanish,[3] and Italian,[4] and he has indeed achieved posthumous international status as a poet. Yet he is virtually unknown in the Anglo-Saxon world, and this is not only regrettable, it is ironical, for Pessoa was educated in South Africa, was bilingual in Portuguese and English, wrote some of his poems in English, and could have translated his own works, had he chosen to do so. Critical studies of his work, now

[1] By Armand Guibert in the series 'Poètes d'aujourd'hui' (no. 73), Paris, Seghers, 1960, and more recently by Sophia de Mello Breyner in *Quatre poètes portugais,* Paris, Presses universitaires de France, 1970, pp. 155-327.
[2] By Georg Rudolf Lind, Frankfurt, Fischer-Verlag, 1965.
[3] By Octavio Paz, Universidad Nacional Autónoma de México 1962.
[4] By Luigi Panarese, Milan, Lerici Editori, 1967.

extremely numerous, are mainly in Portuguese, and the rare items in French, and even rarer items in English, are not easily accessible to the English-speaking reader, being for the most part published abroad in small editions or in little-known periodicals.

Pessoa's poetic achievement is a remarkable one. His verse may not be to everyone's taste, but the preoccupations, doubts and fears which he expresses are very much of our own time. At least a selection of his Portuguese poems, translated into English, and a brief introductory study of the man and his work, now seem called for and indeed overdue.

In the preparation of this book, I have enjoyed the help and encouragement of many. It is a great pleasure to record my gratitude to Sr José Avelino Lima de Faria and Sra D. Maria Natália Lima de Faria, who first introduced me to Pessoa's work, and encouraged me to translate some of the poems; to Sra D. Henriqueta Madalena Rosa Dias and the late Sr Coronel Francisco Caetano Dias, the poet's sister and brother-in-law, for their great kindness in allowing me to consult Pessoa's books and manuscripts; to Sr Francisco Eduardo Guedes Quintanilha, for many fruitful consultations and discussions; to Dr Alison Fairlie of Girton College and Mr Edward Sands of Emmanuel College, for their valuable criticisms of the Introduction; and to Sra Lia Noémia Rodrigues Correia of Darwin College for her patience, her kindness and her ingenuity in helping me to solve a great many difficulties of translation, and for saving me from more blunders than I care to remember.

P. R.

Emmanuel College, Cambridge.

April 1971.

NOTE: Unless otherwise stated, references are to the texts as printed in the 8-volume Ática edition, and all quotations, and indeed all complete poems are reproduced from that edition, as corrected where relevant by comparison with the earliest published versions of the same poems. It should be added that neither edition follows the poet's orthography, since the official spelling of Portuguese was reformed after his death, and is moreover somewhat different in its Brazilian and in its European forms.

A NOTE ON THE TRANSLATIONS

The Portuguese text, printed on the left-hand page, may convey to the reader, through French or Latin, some idea of the poet's choice of words. What it cannot convey is the sound of the language. To assume that, written as it is, and looking conspicuously neo-Latin, Portuguese must sound like Spanish or Italian, is a major error. Pronounced rapidly, the Portuguese of Lisbon does not sound remotely like either. It lacks the crisply articulated, staccato quality of Spanish or Italian. Though it is in fact far richer in vowel sounds, it produces a curiously muffled impression. This is due above all to the relaxed articulation, to the frequent contraction of the syllables leading up to the tonic stress, and to the weakness of those which follow it. Hearing it without the text, one would not easily guess that it is a Romance language, and hearing it with the text, one would at first have some difficulty in finding the place on the page. Portuguese words on the whole have more syllables than English ones, though some of its syllables are regularly 'swallowed'; and the final unstressed syllables are an important sound effect of the language. English is particularly rich in monosyllables, and a great many English words end rather abruptly. Faced with Portuguese lines containing a number of polysyllabic words, coupled with elaborate and sometimes repetitive grammatical constructions, one is tempted to be briefer and more elliptical in English, and this could easily lead to translations which would seem terse and even laconic by comparison. On the other hand, to compensate for this by padding the line would be to do less than justice to Pessoa. Some commonplace Portuguese constructions—the personal infinitive, certain types of causal construction and of noun clause—are admirably neat in Portuguese, but become extremely heavy and prosaic in English, if the translator tries to maintain the construction. He should obviously not carry literalism to such lengths. The difference between *ser* ('to be, essentially') and *estar* ('to be, accidentally') is a notorious difficulty of translation, and Pessoa can be relied on to use the verb one would least expect.

The differences in style between the heteronyms can to some extent be reflected in translation. To take the two extreme cases, Álvaro de Campos and Ricardo Reis. Campos writes in sprawling lines of uneven length, using somewhat colloquial language, and often repeating himself, or ringing the changes on a basic theme, for effect. All this can of course be echoed in English, and, to mention just one possibility, the colloquial verbal contractions of English (*don't, hasn't, I'd, he'll* etc), though they have no equivalent in Portuguese, do not seem out of place in rendering his style. Reis, on the other hand, calls for an archaic and high-flown English, with frequent inversions. Even so, it is difficult to take in English the liberties which Reis takes with word-order, and one is forced to settle for a compromise. Even Portuguese readers are sometimes initially baffled by Reis's word-order.

Fernando Pessoa

INTRODUCTION

THE LIFE. Fernando António Nogueira Pessoa was born in Lisbon on 13 June 1888. His father, Joaquim de Seabra Pessoa, was the son of an infantry lieutenant who eventually became a general and was in turn descended from a Jewish convert to Christianity, whose goods were confiscated by the Inquisition in 1706. He was a member of the editorial staff of the newspaper *Diário de Notícias*, and was its music critic. He had received no higher education, but had largely educated himself, making a special study of musicology, and had even published an opuscule on Wagner's *Flying Dutchman*. The poet's mother, Maria Madalena Pinheiro Nogueira, came from a cultured family domiciled in the island of Terceira in the Azores. The pair married in 1887, when he was thirty-seven and she twenty-five. He was consumptive, and died on 13 July 1893 at the age of forty-three, when the future poet was just five years old. In December of the following year, Maria was married by proxy to Comandante João Miguel Rosa, whom she had met not long after her husband's death and who had just taken up an appointment as Portuguese consul in Durban, South Africa. Mother and son sailed for South Africa a few days later and took up residence in their new home.

After attending a convent school for three years, Fernando entered Durban High School in April 1899. In August 1901, when his step-father had qualified for a year's leave, the family returned to Portugal, and also visited the mother's relatives in the Azores, returning to South Africa in September 1902. Fernando did not at first go back to the High School: instead, he attended the Commercial School, where he acquired that knowledge of business transactions and of commercial correspondence which was later to be his principal source of income. Only in February 1904 did he resume his studies at the High School, but, before doing so, he took the entrance examination for the University of the Cape, in which one of the requirements was, not surprisingly, an English essay. A prize had just been instituted for the best candidate in this paper, and the Queen Victoria Memorial Prize, as it was called, was awarded, for the first time ever, to this Portuguese boy who had learned English as a foreign language. There were nearly nine hundred candidates. In December of the same year, he passed the Intermediate Examination of the University of the Cape, but it was soon decided that he should seek higher education in Portugal. He left South Africa, for ever, in August 1905 at the age of seventeen, returning alone to Lisbon, where he went to live with his two aunts. Also living with them at this time was his paternal grandmother, Dionísia, who had lived with the Pessoas in the old days, before his father's death, and who even then had shown unmistakable signs of insanity. By the time of Fernando's return to Lisbon, she was hopelessly insane.

For a year the young man studied privately in his new home. When, in October 1906, his stepfather and the rest of the family (his mother and the daughter and two sons of her second marriage) arrived in Lisbon on a year's leave, Fernando went to live with them. It was at this time that he matriculated at the University of Lisbon and began a course in literature, which he abandoned in the following year, when the students went on strike as a protest against a measure taken by the dictator João Franco. It was at first his ambition to set up a printing press and to publish his own writings and those of others. He accordingly invested his small capital in a venture called *Empresa Íbis*, but this proved in a very few months to be an expensive failure. For a livelihood, he then turned to the thing for which he was on paper best qualified—commercial correspondence, more particularly foreign correspondence. He had, after all, attended a commercial school, he was bilingual in Portuguese and English, and he also had an excellent knowledge of French, acquired from his mother and from his school-days in South Africa. From 1908 to 1935, the year of his death, he earned a living by working for various commercial houses in Lisbon, often for several at the same time, coming and going much as he pleased, and doing as much routine work of this kind as enabled him to live modestly but comfortably, while leaving him time to indulge his literary interests. When his step-father died in South Africa in October 1919, his mother, sister and two brothers returned to Lisbon, and he went to live with them. His two brothers soon left Portugal for England, where they settled, and his sister married and left home. His mother died in 1925, and thereafter he lived alone, though in everyday contact with other members of his family, particularly his sister and brother-in-law. From time to time he was offered posts far more remunerative than the almost casual employment which he seemed to prefer, but he resolutely declined them, feeling that they would take up too much of his time. The only post he applied for, late in life, was the sinecure of curator of the museum and library at Cascais, the resort and fishing port at the mouth of the Tagus. This was in 1932. His application was unsuccessful.

He never married. In 1920 he carried on a brief courtship with a girl typist in one of the offices where he worked, but nothing came of it: they parted without rancour, and it is clear from letters they exchanged nine years later that they greatly respected each other.

After his return from South Africa, he never left Portugal again: indeed, he did not even stray far from Lisbon, if we except one visit to Portalegre and one to Évora (both in Alentejo). He seldom went further afield than Sintra, or Cascais, or Estoril (where his brother-in-law and sister lived), or the outlying suburbs of his native city.

He died of cirrhosis of the liver on 30 November 1935, aged forty-seven.

Considering that he belongs to the twentieth century, Pessoa is in many ways a surprisingly shadowy figure. Those who met him nearly every day and discussed literature with him in such Lisbon cafés as the *Brasileira* or the *Martinho* liked and admired him, but were somewhat puzzled by the content of his verse, because it did not seem to correspond with what they knew of him as a person; while many of those who met him in his capacity of commercial correspondent had no idea that he wrote poetry. Nevertheless, he takes shape at a certain superficial level which does little if anything to explain his works. A rather unusual gait, rather jerky movements of the hands, rimless or gold-rimmed spectacles, a small moustache over a tiny mouth, neatness and even elegance in dress. Very gentlemanly, exquisitely courteous, chastened in speech, a good listener, a heavy smoker and an increasingly heavy drinker, this last the cause of his early death. A nervous, shoulder-shaking laugh. Though deeply introspective and introverted, he was by no means selfish, and there were many occasions when he put himself to expense and inconvenience to oblige others. He was always ready to contribute a preface to a slim volume of verse by an aspiring young poet, and as an editor—perhaps the ultimate in unselfishness—he would even pass over his own poems in favour of those of someone else. A subtle and witty conversationalist, without *gaucherie* on the one hand, and with nothing of the *poseur* on the other: he was capable of exhibitionism in his writings, but not, it seems, in social intercourse. He was not a sociable person at all, at heart, and yet he had a wide circle of friends and acquaintances.

His interests and activities, apart from poetry, may throw some further light upon this curious man. He would not, by the way, have regarded them as 'apart from poetry': for him, they were all related to his poetic vocation. Be that as it may, he was intensely interested in such subjects as astrology, theosophy, occultism, magic, and freemasonry—in the mysterious, the esoteric, the metaphysical and the supernatural. At one time he believed he possessed mediumistic powers, and in 1916 he seriously thought of setting up as a professional astrologer. His liking for mystery also led him to interest himself in detective fiction, and he even wrote a few stories of crime detection, in which the central character was a certain Dr Quaresma. None of these was published, or even completed. He took freemasonry very seriously, and when, early in 1935, the National Assembly drafted a law banning secret societies, Pessoa passionately defended them—particularly freemasonry—in an article in the *Diário de Lisboa*. His interest in theosophy led him to translate into Portuguese, between 1916 and 1926, several of the works of Annie Besant and of Charles Webster Leadbeater.

It is not surprising that he should have translated some of the poems he most admired, in his desire to make them better known. Thus he translated Edgar Allan Poe's *The Raven*, *Ulalume* and *Annabel Lee*[1] and, because of its particular interest for Portuguese readers, Elizabeth Barrett Browning's *Catarina to Camoens*. More questionably, perhaps, he also translated Aleister Crowley's *Hymn to Pan*.[2] Portuguese poems translated into English include Camoens' sonnet *Alma minha gentil*, and a total of eighty-nine poems by António Botto.

He was a frequent contributor of critical articles and literary appreciations to various journals, published in Lisbon, Coimbra and Oporto: indeed, he was far less diffident about publishing his literary theories than he was about publishing his own poems. He did not shirk editorial duties and responsibilities. He edited the second and third numbers of the review *Orpheu* in 1915–16 (it was not his fault that the third number never came out), and he founded and edited with Ruy Vaz the literary review *Athena*, of which five numbers appeared between October 1924 and February 1925. Among his non-literary activities, he founded and edited, from 1926 onwards, in partnership with his brother-in-law Colonel (then Captain) Francisco Caetano Dias, a journal of commerce and accountancy to which he was frequent contributor. He also patented a commercial directory of his own devising. Although his youthful venture the *Empresa Íbis* was a failure, he had more success with 'Olisipo', the publishing house which he founded in 1921, and by means of which he published some of his English poems, and several volumes of the poems of others. From 1929 onwards, he also edited the works of several modern Portuguese poets in the review *Solução Editora*.

He did not remain consistently aloof from politics: there were occasions when particular events drew from him virulent and at times tactless articles. His most noteworthy interventions, apart from his defence of freemasonry in 1935, occurred in 1915, when he incurred a certain amount of opprobrium for an ill-advised reference to an accident in which a minister had been seriously injured; and in 1928, when he justified military dictatorship, at least as an interim measure, in a pamphlet entitled *O Interregno*.

It is notoriously difficult to account for a person's character. The professional psycho-analyst has been known to have difficulties with a living subject: how much more difficult for the layman when the subject is dead! Unfortunately the biographer of Pessoa, Dr João Gaspar Simões, impressed by certain superficial resemblances between Pessoa's 'case' and that of Charles Baudelaire, has given the poet and his works a strongly Freudian and even Oedipean interpretation. It is possible, of course, that the loss of his father when he was five years old, his mother's remarriage little more than a year later, and the growing insanity of his grandmother when he was at an impressionable age, may go some way towards accounting for his withdrawn and introspective nature. This can only be conjecture, but at all events the analogy with Baudelaire clearly breaks down on one fundamental issue. The severity of Baudelaire's mother, and his step-father's disapproval of the young man's literary career, led to bitterness and estrangement. Pessoa's family did not oppose his literary career, and there was no bitterness or estrangement. He always remained on affectionate terms with his stepfather, with his mother, with the children of her second marriage, and with his stepfather's brother, General Henrique Rosa who, after the young man's return to Portugal, did much to encourage him in his poetic career.

What we know of his life in society does next to nothing to explain his poetry, and very little to explain his prose. For the interpretation of his poetry, it is his inner life which is all-important, and of that we know nothing except what he tells us in his poetry, and what he chose to reveal in letters.

EXPLORATION AND SELF-DISCOVERY. It must be admitted that Pessoa had certain initial advantages. His mother and father were both of cultured and literary tastes. His mother spoke French, and wrote Portuguese verse: one of his mother's aunts, Maria Xavier Rinheiro da Cunha, who was devoted to the boy, specialized in elegant Arcadian sonnets of a kind which had been extremely fashionable in Portugal in the eighteenth century, and for which there was still a certain vogue in the nineteenth. The uncle he acquired when his mother remarried, the retired general of engineers Henrique Rosa, also wrote sonnets, some of which Pessoa later published.[3] Both in Lisbon and in Durban, the family home was well equipped with books. The boy's first recorded poem is a quatrain dated 26 July 1895, a simple comment on the imminent departure of mother and son for a new life in South Africa. It is entitled *To my dear mamma* and reads: 'Though I love this land, this land where I was born, yet you I love more dearly'.

Long afterwards, in a famous letter about which more will be said later, he claimed that one of his earliest childhood memories was that at the age of six he had written letters to himself signed 'Le Chevalier de Pas', and he thought there was someone else, also with a foreign name, who was a rival of the Chevalier.[4] Nothing is more normal in children than a tendency to pretend and to make believe, yet even so, this precocious letter-writing suggests something deeper, a conscious and deliberate identification with an imagined person, highly significant for Pessoa's later development.

In South Africa, he encountered the English language and English literature—Shakespeare, Milton, Dickens, Wordsworth, and the romantic poets, particularly Shelley. He also studied Latin and French at school, his French being further supported at home by his mother's knowledge of the language. He seems to have rapidly overcome the initial disadvantage of having to compete with boys for whom English, the medium of instruction at school, was their native tongue. Indeed, it is certain that the study of English, and its daily use, heightened his linguistic awareness, giving him a deeper insight into the language he spoke at home and suggesting new possibilities for linguistic and stylistic innovation in Portuguese. The English essay for which he was awarded the Queen Victoria Memorial Prize in February 1904[5] has unfortunately not survived, but in December of the same year, an essay on Macaulay by Fernando Pessoa appeared in the Durban High School Magazine.[6] In this essay, based on wide reading, there are clear signs of a remarkable and precocious critical insight, together with a marked ability to detect and formulate subtle distinctions. The style has a bookish and somewhat archaic flavour, and contains some rather startling neologisms such as 'sky-disturbance' and 'thunder-march', indicating a taste for word-creation which was to leave ample traces in his later poetry, both English and Portuguese. In South Africa, and indeed until 1909, four years after his return to Portugal, he appears to have written poetry exclusively in English. The only exception is a short poem which he composed during the family's visit to the Azores in May 1902. In this poem, entitled 'When she passes by', he manages to suggest a sense of loss by subtle use of the contrast between past and present. It is typical of Pessoa that the one poem he wrote in the Azores should have nothing to do with exotic scenery or with the sea. In just the same way, the poetry he wrote in South Africa does not reflect South Africa in any obvious way, and the poetry he wrote in Lisbon only rarely refers to city life, and then only with extreme vagueness. Throughout his poetic life, Pessoa was to seek inspiration from within himself rather than from his material surroundings.

From the period 1903 to 1909, no fewer than 107 English poems survive, and it is clear from lists which have been found that many more were written which were subsequently lost, or were perhaps destroyed by the poet himself. Several of the surviving poems, signed 'Alexander Search'—the name he adopted for the English poems of this period—have recently been published, complete or in extract.[7] They are of uneven value, but from time to time they contain striking anticipations of his later Portuguese poems. I do not propose to comment further here on these points of resemblance: I shall however in the notes to the Portuguese poems which follow, occasionally refer to and quote from specific English poems belonging to this early period. It should also be remarked at this stage that although Pessoa wrote poems in both languages, he wrote far more in Portuguese than in English, and furthermore *never* translated any of his English poems into Portuguese, or any of his Portuguese poems into English. He appears either to have made a conscious choice of language in each case or to have composed instinctively in one language rather than the other. Certainly one can relate his Portuguese poems to his English poems, and vice versa, though far more themes are treated in Portuguese than in English, and one can discern numerous images and conceits which are shared by both groups of poems, but the poems are never the same. The Portuguese poems sometimes contain a distant echo of the English ones, but they never repeat them.

It was only after he had been living in Portugal again for

four years that he began to write poetry in Portuguese. In February 1909 he wrote six sonnets bearing the collective title *In search of beauty*, a commentary on a poem by the symbolist poet Eugénio de Castro.[8] The theme, profoundly pessimistic, is that the quest for beauty, for perfection, is not only a torment, it is utterly vain. Let us, rather, seek complete detachment and total renunciation:

'With folded arms, with neither thought nor faith
Let us forswear all sorrow, all desire . . .' (no. 5)

Even the oblivion of sleep is illusory: the only remedy is to aspire to nothing, and even then life will be a living hell of boredom. The utter scepticism, the hopelessness which expects nothing from life—so important a theme in Pessoa's later work—is already apparent in this early group of poems. The same theme is later to find expression in many different ways.

For the next three years, Pessoa wrote very little verse, but appears to have read widely, adding to his own collection of books and spending a great deal of his spare time in public libraries, particularly the National Library and the Library of the Academy of Sciences. In a country which had long been orientated towards the French language and culture, his knowledge of English literature, and his experience of an Anglo-Saxon environment, had a certain scarcity value which he was not slow to exploit. It must not be supposed, however, that he neglected or underestimated recent developments in French literature. He was an admirer of French symbolist poetry and was thoroughly familiar with the works of such poets as Baudelaire, Verlaine, Rimbaud, Laforgue and Maeterlinck. By this time, moreover, with or without the encouragement of his uncle Henrique Rosa, he had soaked himself in the Portuguese poetry of the nineteenth century, and had come to know what was best in such poets as Antero de Quental (1842–91), Almeida Garrett (1799–1854), Cesário Verde (1855–86), António Nobre (1867–1900) and—still alive at this period of Pessoa's life—Gomes Leal (1848–1921). It is indeed probable that his eccentric uncle helped to determine his orientation, or to confirm him in latent tendencies. At all events, it is a remarkable coincidence that a man like Fernando Pessoa should have met a man like Henrique Rosa. The ex-general was a man of wide culture and insatiable intellectual curiosity, as widely read in science as in literature. For long periods he would withdraw from circulation altogether and take to his bed, imagining that he was ill. Then suddenly, perhaps several months later, he would appear again and be the life and soul of café society. An extreme pessimist with the lowest possible view of human nature, he may also have appealed to Pessoa as the living personification of his own ideal of the self-sufficient, solitary individual. Rosa's own poetry was not very distinguished, but at least it was always thoughtful, and carefully elaborated.

At all events, by 1912 Pessoa had absorbed most of the influences which, filtered through his complex personality, were to give his work its characteristic stamp. Much has been made of the alleged influence upon him of the pseudo-philosophical treatise on degeneracy by Max Nordau,[9] a work which he read in a French translation, probably in 1907 or 1908. This was a wide-ranging and almost pathological attack on the alleged degeneracy of nineteenth-century European literature, art and thought. Tolstoy, Wagner, Ibsen, Nietzsche, the English Pre-Raphaelites and the French symbolists and naturalists were declared by Nordau to be just so many feeble-minded degenerates. It is certain that Pessoa, who had an extremely open mind where literary movements were concerned, did not share this view. Indeed, in a manuscript note probably to be dated 1913,[10] we find the poet pointing out in no uncertain terms the glaring fallacy of Nordau's thesis, that, in short, of confusing progress with regression. One could indeed, if one wished, regard symbolism as 'decadent romanticism', but that would be a purely negative definition of it, and Pessoa clearly saw, as Nordau did not, the positive achievements of that movement, and appreciated its importance as an artistic expression of the thoughts and aspirations of modern man. If he had any reservations about French symbolism, they were surely not due to Nordau. This is of course not to deny that Nordau may have influenced him in a quite different way, by convincing him that he shared at least some of the allegedly degenerate symptoms which Nordau so readily attributed to the objects of his attack, namely suggestibility, hypersensitivity, and a readiness to believe in their own fantasies. What Pessoa most appreciated in recent symbolist poetry was its resolute opposition to realism, its subtlety, its polyvalence, its power to suggest without describing, for all this accorded admirably with his own poetic instincts. The belief in a transcendental reality beyond appearances, suggested by Baudelaire's sonnet *Correspondances*, was shared by Pessoa, and though there are traces of this belief in some of the early poems which he wrote in English, it was to become fundamental to his later poetry. By 1912, the young man was exceptionally well read in English, French and Portuguese literature, and was now as completely at home in Lisbon as he could ever be anywhere. He began to feel that he had a contribution to make both to the theory and to the practice of poetry in Portugal. At this time, Portuguese poetry was still following, in the main, the twin currents of its nineteenth-century tradition: on the one hand, pretentious rhetoric, and on the other, sentimental lyricism. There had, however, been some notable exceptions: Antero de Quental, famous for his deeply spiritual sonnets; Cesário Verde, appreciated above all for his sensitive presentations of everyday reality; Eugénio de Castro, profoundly imbued with French symbolism; and António Nobre, so strikingly modern in his treatment of traditional themes. All these were appreciated by Pessoa. But Lisbon at this time was a backwater far removed from the main stream of European culture, and foreign influences were greatly diluted, if not actively resisted, as they were by such poets as Teixeira de Pascoais, who placed the emphasis on the traditional Portuguese quality of *saudosismo* —the literary cult of *saudade* or yearning. That a certain element of *saudosismo* is not incompatible with new ideas was something which Pessoa was later to demonstrate. Be that as it may, Portugal, in the years immediately preceding the First World War, was ripe for poetic renovation.

In December 1910, a literary journal named *A Águia* ('The Eagle') had been founded in Oporto, and this soon became the organ of a literary society known as *Renascença Portuguesa* ('Portuguese Renaissance'). To this journal Pessoa contributed a series of critical articles in 1912:[11] two on the theme 'The new Portuguese poetry viewed sociologically' (nos. 4 and 5), and three entitled 'The psychological aspect of the new Portuguese poetry' (nos. 9, 11 and 12). In the first two articles, he expressed his confidence that Portugal would soon produce a great poet—a 'super-Camoens' as he called him—and would have an important contribution to make to European culture, indeed, a message for humanity. The most important theme to emerge from the other three articles is his conviction that the most notable and original feature of the new Portuguese poetry will be the quest for 'em tudo um Além'—a transcendental quality in everything. In this he was in fact describing his own literary preferences, and insisting on what he knew to be his own strong point, though it should be added that his prophecies were vindicated, not only in himself, but in others too, and in none so strikingly as in his close friend Mário de Sá-Carneiro. By the following year, Pessoa was also contributing articles to the Lisbon journal *Teatro*, though in a quite different vein. Here irony, mockery and irreverence are the dominant note. A tone of high seriousness had characterized his earlier articles in *A Águia*.

By this time the young poet was in close contact with other poets such as Armando Cortes-Rodrigues, Alfredo Pedro Guisado, Raul Leal and many others, and was an *habitué* of cafés like the *Brasileira* and the *Martinho*, where such strikingly new literary and artistic trends as cubism and futurism were discussed, and where poems were compared and commented on. The main current of influence from outside was, however, that of the French post-symbolists. In 1913, Pessoa wrote some of the poems which, when they were published, first heralded his greatness, though they were written at least in part to startle and to scandalize the staid Lisbon *bourgeoisie*, considered with some justification to be narrow, backward-looking, and completely out of touch with recent developments outside Portugal. In his wish to startle and shock, Pessoa was not alone. Although such an ambition is not incompatible with real talent, it is a fact that the young generation of poets meeting in the cafés of the 'Baixa' or business quarter of Lisbon wanted to draw attention to themselves. They did not expect to be understood by those whom they regarded as philistines, and therefore thought they might as well be hanged for sheep as for lambs. Hence an element of wilful obscurity and mystification, side by side with a sincere wish to renovate the national literature and to compete seriously with that of other countries.

In February 1914, a new journal appeared in Lisbon, entitled *A Renascença* ('The Renaissance'), the renaissance in question being of course the imminent or actual rebirth of Portuguese poetry. It contained two poems by Fernando Pessoa, under the title 'Twilight Impressions'. The first of these, *Paùis* ('Quagmires'), was to give its name to *paùlismo*, the new poetic ideal of the young generation. It consists of a riot of apparently disconnected images, with an irregularly recurring interaction of abstract and concrete, and a startling juxtaposition of ideas and even of parts of speech, while it nevertheless contrives to suggest, subtly and unobtrusively, a connection between the poet's soul and material reality. In lines like 'A fleshly chill pervades my soul' and 'The Mystery tastes of my being Another'[12] we can already see something of Pessoa's metaphysical preoccupation, side by side with his love of disconcerting contrasts between two levels of awareness. This style was imitated by those who believed in it, and mercilessly pastiched by those who did not, and who saw in it something facile, deliberately inconsequential, and spuriously pregnant. The second poem *Ó sino da minha aldeia* ('Oh church bell in my village') has stood the test of time much better. It is a simpler poem, though by no means lacking in subtlety, and its message emerges far more clearly. The reality of the village bell is greatly attenuated: what matters in the poem, and what receives the emphasis, is the effect of its tolling on the poet's psyche. Indeed, at a certain moment the very reality of its tolling is called into doubt.

No further numbers of *A Renascença* appeared, but soon a new journal was being planned, to be published in Portugal and in Brazil simultaneously, under the joint editorship of Luís de Montalvor (Portugal) and Ronald de Carvalho (Brazil). It was to be entitled *Orpheu. A literary quarterly*. Its aim was basically to give poetic or at least literary expression to things hitherto considered inexpressible—inexpressible not because good taste forbade expression (the *Orpheu* generation was not interested in crude realism), but because of the limitations of language itself, and of the power of association. The first number appeared in April 1915,[13] and contained poems by Mário de Sá-Carneiro, Ronald de Carvalho, Alfredo Pedro Guisado, Armando Cortes-Rodrigues, and one 'Álvaro de Campos'. This last was Fernando Pessoa, who also contributed in his own name a 'dramatic poem in prose' entitled 'The Sailor'. 'Álvaro de Campos'—more will be said later about the name Pessoa adopted—contributed two poems, *Opiário* and *Ode Triunfal* ('Triumphal Ode'), the first in rhyming four-line stanzas, the second in *vers libre*. In the first, we have to suppose that the poet, a drug-addict, is passing through the Suez Canal in a ship, utterly bored and convinced that life has nothing to offer but the same mortal *ennui* wherever one goes. He longs for death, and when he exclaims 'God change my life or end it', one has the feeling that it is the latter alternative which he would prefer. The theme of the poem is what the Portuguese call *tédio*—world-weariness and disgust with life—a theme common enough in the Portuguese poetry of the period, but here given an extreme and disconcerting expression. 'Triumphal Ode' strikes a very unconventional note, and we do not have to read far to recognize the influence of Walt Whitman, whom Pessoa greatly admired at this time. The poet sings enthusiastically, and even feverishly, of modern machinery, the noise, vibration and glaring light of the factory, suggesting that the machine age is the new classical age. Apostrophe and enumeration *à la* Whitman help to give this poem a breathless, dynamic quality which is in harmony with its theme. A masochistic note is struck when Campos, in his eagerness to identify himself with the world of machines, hopes to be crushed and destroyed by them. Half-way, the emphasis shifts to the miseries of mankind, but there is no trace, in the poet's attitude, of pity or of moral indignation. Then, after a reminder that we must all die, Campos turns back again to modern machinery, this time again stressing its destructiveness, and evoking accidents, disasters, and wars. If at the beginning of the poem he wanted to be at one with machines, at the end this wish appears to be fulfilled: indeed, he goes further and identifies himself with such basic sources of energy as steam and electricity. But the last line expresses a regret that he cannot simultaneously be everybody everywhere.

It is poems such as these, together with Sá-Carneiro's strange sonnet 'Apotheosis' and Cortes-Rodrigues' mystical poem 'Other', which account for the *succès de scandale* of *Orpheu*. The press reacted violently, as the contributors all hoped it would, and some critics even suggested that the *Orpheu* poets were insane. The group had aimed at jolting the public out of its complacency, and in that it was conspicuously successful. Certainly there was in the first number of *Orpheu* a strong element of pose, of exhibitionism, of the desire to shock bourgeois preconceptions of poetry; but there was also considerable talent and originality, and a promise of better things to come. Pessoa and the others felt encouraged, at all events, to go ahead with their plans for the next number. When it appeared, on 28 June 1915, it contained a long poem —some thirty pages—by 'Álvaro de Campos', once again showing clear traces of the influence of Walt Whitman, and entitled 'Maritime Ode', a poem which Roy Campbell has described as 'the loudest ever written'.[14] It was hardly calculated to reassure the press or the *bourgeoisie:* on the contrary, it was far more likely to confirm them in their worst suspicions. The beginning of the poem is a perfectly straightforward description of a situation. Campos is standing on a deserted quay watching a ship come in. But soon he begins to feel as if he were someone else, as if one day long ago he had sailed from such a quay. Reality intervenes from time to time as the ship comes nearer, but Campos falls into a profound reverie and begins to *live* in his imagination all the associations the sea suggests to him, while at the same time he retains some intermittent awareness that he is a civilized person, an engineer standing on a quay in Lisbon. Gradually the imagination takes control as he feels a revulsion from the narrowness of his life. He evokes all the violence of which the sea—and sailors—are capable: he longs to have experienced all the storms, sea-battles and discoveries of the past, to have been at once the pirate and the pirate's victims. It is here that he falls into Whitmanesque apostrophes and enumerations, punctuated by screams, loud cries of 'ship ahoy!', and snatches of sea-shanties—these last in English. The poem ends on a quiet note as a ship gradually passes out of sight. Longer, far longer than 'Triumphal Ode', 'Maritime Ode' cannot really be described as incoherent, for it retains a certain loose structural unity, and there are many calculated and balanced effects. It is basically a particular way of looking at the sea and dreaming about it, and at the same time there is that interplay of imagination and reality, waking and dreaming, which Pessoa could suggest so skilfully. Another theme in this poem, discreetly present and not seriously disturbing its unity, is the idea that the *modern* world of machines and steamships is also entitled to poetic expression—an idea which was gaining ground among the *Orpheu* group, as the futurist ideas of Marinetti slowly filtered through from Paris.

To the same number of *Orpheu*, Pessoa contributed in his own name six poems under the general title of *Chuva oblíqua* ('Slanting Rain'). These poems can hardly be said to tell a story. Each one vaguely suggests a particular location, and, within that location, evokes a succession of disconnected images and boldly interrelated incompatibles, for example a landscape *and ships*: 'and the ships pass into the tree-trunks,/ vertically horizontal/and drop their moorings into the water through the leaves, one by one' . . . 'Trees, stones, hills, are *dancing motionless* within me' . . . 'And the windows of the church seen from outside are the sound of the rain heard from inside'. If 'Maritime Ode' contained suggestions of futurism, 'Slanting Rain' typifies what came to be known as *inter-seccionismo*, the attempt to express several imaginary sensations at once, deliberately blurring or even omitting relationships of time and space, and leaving in obscurity the links between outer reality and inner experience. Carried to extremes, this could mean complete disregard for logic, coherence and even grammar.

With the exception of 'Oh church bell in my village', the Portuguese poems Pessoa had published so far share the quality of extremeness and exaggeration. They were deliberate attempts to go beyond any sort of conventional poetry known in Portugal at the time. In other words, there was a strong element of propaganda and exhibitionism in these published poems. Yet it must be said that by this time, that is by the middle of 1915, he had also written poems of a very different kind, of which the most outstanding example is the one he entitled simply 'Excerpt from an Ode', and which is basically a long apostrophe to Night.[15] He had in fact discovered where his true genius lay. It is precisely the poems which for the most part he did *not* publish at this time, which in the light of his later writings emerge as truly typical of what was best in him. How does one explain this apparent aberration on his part? In one of two ways, or possibly by a combination of the two. He may have doubted whether the public would appreciate them—though this kind of consideration did not prevent him from publishing poems which he must have *known* the public would not appreciate. He may have felt a certain *pudeur* because these poems contained much more of himself than the ones he published, but, most likely, I think, he felt like his generation the need to state an extreme case in print, to create a sensation, to exaggerate in order to open the public mind to new ideas. That he was well aware of the difference between what he regarded as his true literary mission and what he considered mere fringe activities, emerges clearly from a letter which he wrote to his friend and fellow-poet Armando Cortes-Rodrigues on 19 January 1915.[16] Complaining of his spiritual isolation, he wrote 'In no one around me do I find an attitude to life which is in complete harmony with my innermost feelings, with my aspirations and ambitions, with everything which lies at the very root and base of my deepest spiritual being. I can, it is true, find people who are in agreement with literary activities which are merely on the fringe of my true feelings; but that is not enough for me. And so, as my feelings deepen, as I become increasingly aware of the terrible, religious mission which every man of genius receives from God together with his genius, any kind of literary trifling, or art which is merely art, gradually sounds more and more hollow and repugnant to me' . . . 'I have got over the crude desire to shine for the sake of shining, and that other even cruder desire to startle and shock, so unbearably plebeian in an artistic context.'

Soon *Orpheu* was in financial difficulties. The editors were now Fernando Pessoa and Mário de Sá-Carneiro, an extremely gifted young poet, though emotionally unstable and tormented by numerous complexes. Parental pressure forced Sá-Carneiro to give up participation in the venture, and soon afterwards he committed suicide in Paris (26 April 1916) to the utter consternation of Pessoa, who was his closest friend and who felt about poetry as he did. The third number of *Orpheu* was announced, nevertheless, in September 1916, and indeed some of the sheets were actually printed, but it was never published. That particular venture was at an end.

All this time, quite apart from his activities as a commercial correspondent, Pessoa was writing articles on literary criticism. In these he displayed an urgent wish to persuade (which helps to explain why he was so ready to publish criticism while so unwilling, generally speaking, to publish his own poems) and considerable virtuosity in making 'the worse appear the better reason'. Indeed, he always retained the power to demonstrate with equal facility and with irrefragable logic, mutually exclusive propositions. Poems published at this time convey little idea of his real output. Many poems written in 1915 and 1916 were not published until long afterwards, or indeed were not published at all in his lifetime, poems like 'Greetings to Walt Whitman', written by 'Álvaro de Campos' on 11 June 1915, another rather noisy and exclamatory poem; or, the last to show the influence of Whitman, 'The passing of the hours', written in May 1916.

In a review named *Exílio*, published in April 1916—the only number to appear—Pessoa published twenty-five quatrains written nearly three years before, and entitled 'Absurd Hour'. In these he contrives to suggest a mood by almost systematically comparing incomparables: 'My dreams are a staircase with an end but no beginning', 'my idea of you is a corpse washed ashore by the sea', 'your silence is a ship in full sail'. A certain preoccupation with the non-existent can be seen in lines like 'There are so few people who love landscapes which are not' . . . 'the scent chrysanthemums would have if they were scented'. . . . 'I was loved in effigy in a land beyond all dreams'. Dreams and fog, as images of uncertain vision, both mentioned in this group of poems, were to be a recurring theme in Pessoa's later poetry.

But it was in an equally short-lived 'periodical', *Centauro*, published late in 1916, that Fernando Pessoa at last published poems which revealed not just potential and promise, but real greatness. These were fourteen sonnets, composed in 1914 and 1915, to which he gave the name *Passos da Cruz* ('Stations of the Cross')—because there were fourteen of them. The wilful mingling of concrete and abstract, so obtrusive and even systematic in the early poems, is here more selectively applied, and results in images of great beauty and suggestive power. Formally, the poems are perfect, and they abound in memorable lines. The images he devises to express a mood are subtle, yet exquisitely appropriate to each case. *Taedium vitae* finds prominent expression, but also the haunting awareness of something which is out of reach and may not even exist, an impossible ideal. This is expressed, for example, in the fourth sonnet, in which he imagines a woman playing on the harp, and exclaims

> 'Could I but kiss
> The movement of your hands, without the hands themselves'

and in the seventh, where he says

> 'Could I but be, I know not where nor how
> A thing existing though not having life,
> Life's night without its dawning . . .'

In another striking sonnet, the sixth, he compares himself with the *backward glance* of Boabdil, the last Moorish king, as he fled from Granada for ever: in other words, he identifies himself with the king's regret for what he has lost, and he even moves on to a yet bolder identification:

> 'I am myself the loss I suffered'[17]

The haunted feeling that he may be merely the medium of some occult power, whose influence he is powerless to resist, and that he has no independent existence, finds expression in no. XI:

> 'Not I describe myself. I am the canvas:
> On me a hidden hand paints Someone'[18]

while in the best-known and most memorable of these poems, no. XIII, he begins

> 'Sent as the envoy of an unknown king
> I carry out vague promptings from beyond'[19]

and though he goes on to doubt whether the unknown king even exists, he still considers that he has a mission to fulfil, which cuts him off from other men.

As we have seen, Pessoa already felt—and indeed in the *Centauro* poems showed—that he was not really in harmony with any literary trend or school or '-ism', however fashionable. Yet it is a fact that he allowed himself to become involved in the literary manifestations of the futurist movement in Portugal. The chief publicists for this movement in Portugal were Guilherme de Santa Rita, known as Santa Rita Pintor, who brought from Paris the futurist message of Marinetti, and José de Almada-Negreiros. Santa Rita had no real talent as a painter, but was a flamboyant exhibitionist with a genius for publicity. Almada-Negreiros, on the other hand, was extremely gifted and versatile, as a painter,[20] as a caricaturist, and as a man of letters. He began by attacking conventional

academic literary values, as typified by Júlio Dantas, in an
'Anti-Dantas Manifesto'. He followed this up, in April 1917,
with a public lecture in a Lisbon theatre, proclaiming the
futurist movement as already, in effect, triumphant over the
hitherto fashionable Portuguese *saudosismo* or (literary)
regret for the past. It seemed appropriate that such a move-
ment should have its own organ, and so the first (and, as it
happened, the last) number of *Portugal Futurista* appeared
in December 1917. It was promptly seized by the police,
because of the indecent language used by Almada-Negreiros
in the part which he contributed. 'Álvaro de Campos', i.e.
Pessoa, contributed an article entitled *Ultimatum*, a scathing
denunciation of the mediocrity of men of letters and even of
statesmen, in several countries, applying to them contemp-
tuous nicknames and adding the peremptory demand that
they should get out and make way for their betters.[21] The true
artist, says Campos, should be capable of feeling for others,
past, present and future, who are *unlike* himself—a highly
significant remark in the light of Pessoa's development.
Portugal Futurista also contained a reminder of his versatility
as a poet: two groups of five poems entitled respectively
'Fictions in the Interlude' and 'Episodes. The Mummy'. The
first five poems, in rhyme, are remarkable as a *tour de force* of
elaborate word-play and alliteration, embroidering a theme of
light-hearted fantasy. 'The Mummy', in *vers libre*, is a remark-
ably successful attempt to create an atmosphere of growing
terror. As in some of his earlier poems, the very concepts of
time and space are undermined.

'I walked leagues of shadow
 Within my thought . . .'
'I suddenly forgot
 What space is like, and time
   Instead of horizontal
   Is vertical . . .'

The poet walks in terror among inanimate objects which
conceal the Unknown:

'Why do things open their ranks for me to pass?
 I dare not pass between them, so still and aware,
 I dare not leave them behind me taking off their
   Masks . . .

. . . .

I feel their *eyeless gaze* upon me, and I shudder . . .
Without moving, the walls *hurl meaning at me* . . .
Where are they looking at me *from*?
What things *incapable of looking* are looking at me?
Who is watching it all?'

In 'The Mummy', then, we find already a vivid expression of the metaphysical doubts and fears which were to play so important a part in Pessoa's inspiration. He doubts the reality of things, or rather, he discerns different levels or layers of reality. Surely what we see cannot be the ultimate: there must be something else? He longs to probe the mystery, but is at the same time terrified of what he may find.

We have now followed some, but not all, of the directions of Pessoa's literary development up to 1917, and we know from the letter to Cortes-Rodrigues that already in January 1915 he had come to realize the true nature of his poetic mission. It was this realization which led him henceforward to abandon the fashionable exaggerations and the cult of the sensational, in order the better to tap the deep wells of inspiration which he had discovered within himself.

THE GENESIS OF THE HETERONYMS. From 1912 to 1917, Pessoa, in his wish to help to promote a renovation of the national literature, had given an enthusiastic welcome to new ideas, whatever their provenance, and had helped to launch them and publicize them as a critic as well as to demonstrate them, in a modified form, in his own verse. Yet his keenly critical faculties and his own poetic temperament did not allow him to identify himself with any one literary movement, whether of foreign origin or not. Indeed, it might be said that a heightened awareness of the literary values of others gave him a keener insight into his own poetic strength and weakness. At all events, although for the rest of his life he continued to write critical articles from time to time, and always kept up to date with the latest developments in the poetry of others, he ceased to write poetry to illustrate or to exemplify the tenets of a particular school, and wrote only the kind of poetry he felt a compelling inner urge to write. We have seen that he had undergone a change of heart by 1915, and indeed even earlier. We must now look more closely at that change of heart.

The early poems he wrote in English were attributed to one 'Alexander Search'. Some of the first of his Portuguese poems to be published were, as we have seen, ascribed to 'Álvaro de Campos'. As a matter of fact, by 1915 he had also written, though not published, a great many other poems which he signed with two other names, 'Alberto Caeiro' and 'Ricardo Reis'. Here we touch upon something fundamental to the understanding of his change of heart, and indeed of his works as a whole—the question of the 'heteronyms'. Pessoa always insisted that his 'other names' were no mere pseudonyms of the kind frequently adopted by authors for a variety of reasons —modesty, discretion, convenience or sheer caprice—and in no way affecting their manner of writing or their choice of subject. A pseudonym is merely the use of another name in order to continue to be the same person, in order to go on saying what one would have said in any case. But Álvaro de Campos, Alberto Caeiro and Ricardo Reis (not to mention other less productive heteronyms which appeared later) were, Pessoa maintained, not just names: they were person-alities who produced poetry—and at times prose—in keeping with their education, their temperament, their preoccupations and their philosophy of life. On the other hand, he never tried to suggest seriously (though he sometimes joked about it) that any such persons existed in any material sense. Though he expresses himself on this vexed question in different ways at different times, it seems clear that they were in fact different facets or expressions of his own many-sided personality, or represented conceivable though at times debatable points of view which he could *imagine*, without necessarily approving of them. In intention, at least, and to a considerable extent in achievement, they were all different from each other, and different, individually and collectively, from 'F. P. himself', to use Pessoa's own abbreviation. So it is understandable that he did not consider 'pseudonyms' a suitable term.

An account of the genesis of the heteronyms, and a summary of the characteristics of each, are a necessary preliminary to discussion of the poetry attributed to them and of its relation-ship with that which Pessoa signed with his own name. It is customary to use the terms 'heteronymic' and 'orthonymic' in referring to the two respective groups of poems.

The earliest heteronymic poems were written during the

first half of 1914, and within a year, as we have seen, a few of those attributed to Álvaro de Campos had been published. On 19 January 1915, in a letter to the poet Armando Cortes-Rodrigues,[22] Pessoa throws some light on this question. He speaks of his intention to launch, i.e. publish (for he had already written many of the heteronymic poems) the works of Caeiro, Reis and Campos, 'a whole literature which I created and lived, and which is sincere because it is *felt*. . . . What I call insincere literature is not like that of Alberto Caeiro, Ricardo Reis or Álvaro de Campos. . . . Theirs is written *in the person of another*: it is written *dramatically*, but is sincere (in my serious sense of the word) just as what King Lear says is sincere, although he is not Shakespeare, but a creation of his. I mean by insincere those things which are done in order to astonish people, and also those things which . . . do not contain a basic metaphysical idea, i.e. are not inspired by a sense of the gravity and mystery of Life. For that reason, all I have written in the name of Caeiro, Reis and Campos is serious. In each of them I placed a profound conception of life, a serious involvement with the mysterious importance of Existence'. He goes on to dismiss a poem like 'Quagmires' as not serious, and to condemn his earlier attitude towards the public as that of a clown.

Much of what he said on this occasion is confirmed by a manuscript note which unfortunately cannot be dated:[23] 'For some psychological reason which I do not propose to go into, and which is unimportant, I constructed within myself several characters who are distinct from each other and from me, and to whom I attributed several poems which are not such as I, with my own feelings and ideas, would write. . . . Many of them express ideas I do not accept, and feelings I have never felt. They must simply be read for what they are'. He further argues that no one would challenge Shakespeare's right to create Lady Macbeth on the grounds that he was not a woman, and he claims a similar right for the non-dramatic characters of fiction.

Twenty years later, when Adolfo Casais Monteiro, an admirer and disciple of his, wrote from Coimbra to ask him to account for the origin of the heteronyms, Pessoa replied at some length.[24] This time we learn something about the 'psychological reason' which he had earlier regarded as unimportant and had declined to enlarge upon. Pessoa attributes the need for heteronymy to the element of hysteria, or possibly hystero-neurasthenia in his make-up. He did not mention this in 1915,[25] but he had read Freud, not to mention Max Nordau, and he may have fancied he recognized some of his own symptoms in their descriptions and analyses of hystero-neurasthenic types. It is not necessary to suppose that either Freud or Nordau turned Pessoa into a hystero-neurasthenic: one could perfectly well assume that they simply provided him with a label for something he knew or thought was true of himself. He may have wanted or needed to believe what they had to say. 'Anyway', Pessoa goes on, in his long letter to Casais Monteiro, 'the mental origin of my heteronyms lies in the constant and organic tendency I have towards depersonalization and make-believe. . . . These phenomena [i.e. hysteria or hystero-neurasthenia], luckily for me and for others, have taken on a mental form in me; by that, I mean that they do not show themselves in my practical, outward life in contact with others; they explode inwardly, and I live them alone with myself'.[26] He then explains more particularly how the heteronyms originated:

'Ever since I was a child, I have tended to create around me a fictitious world, to surround myself with friends and acquaintances who never existed. (I don't know, of course, whether they *really* didn't exist, or whether I'm the one who doesn't exist. We mustn't be dogmatic in these matters, or indeed in any others). Ever since I have known myself to be the one I call ME, I can remember giving, in my mind, precise shapes, movements, characters and histories to various unreal figures who were to me just as visible, just as much my own as the phenomena of what we perhaps wrongly call "real life".' As an example of this early tendency, he cites the case of 'Le Chevalier de Pas', already referred to. Then he goes on to relate that around 1912 he had the idea of writing some poems 'of a pagan type'. Although he gave up the idea, at least provisionally, he had formed a picture, in his mind's eye, of the person who wrote such poetry. Though he did not know it at the time, this was the genesis of Ricardo Reis. A year or two later, wishing to play a trick on Mário de Sá-Carneiro, he tried to invent 'a pastoral poet of a complicated type', with a view to passing him off as really existing. He had already given up this project when, on 8 March 1914, feeling suddenly inspired, he took a sheet of paper, and going to a tall chest of drawers, began to write standing up, as was his habit. 'And I wrote more than thirty poems straight off, in a kind of ecstasy which I cannot define . . . I began with a title, *O Guardador de Rebanhos* ('The Keeper of Flocks'). The next thing that happened was that someone appeared to me, to whom I promptly gave the name Alberto Caeiro. I know it sounds absurd, but my master had appeared. That was my immediate reaction. . . . Once Alberto Caeiro had appeared, I soon tried—instinctively and subconsciously—to find disciples for him. I took my potential Ricardo Reis away from his false paganism, I discovered his name, and I made him consistent with himself, because by that time I could *see* him. And suddenly, totally unlike Ricardo Reis in origin, yet another individual occurred vividly to my mind. Spontaneously, on my type-writer, without a break or a correction, the 'Triumphal Ode' of Álvaro de Campos came into being.' . . . Pessoa then relates how he filled in details of the relationship between the three heteronyms, and even suggests that he personally had very little to do with it: it was as though the newly-created personalities had taken over completely. He gives some biographical details about the heteronyms, based on his early vision of them:

Ricardo Reis. Born in Oporto in 1887. A doctor by profession. Educated by Jesuits. Was taught Latin properly and half taught himself Greek. Height a little below average, strong and wiry in build, rather dark complexion. Has lived in Brazil since 1919, in voluntary exile because of monarchist sympathies.

Alberto Caeiro. Born in 1889 in Lisbon, but lived nearly all his life in the country. His parents died when he was a child, and he lived with an elderly aunt. Only primary education. Average height, fair hair, blue eyes. Profession: none. Died of tuberculosis in 1915, aged 26.

Álvaro de Campos. Born in Tavira [Algarve], 15 October 1890. By profession a naval engineer, but at present not active as such. Lives in Lisbon. Tall, thin and slightly stooping. Wears a monocle. Portuguese Jewish type in facial appearance. *Lycée* education. Has travelled widely.

'How do I write in the name of these three?' he asks in

conclusion, echoing the question Casais Monteiro had asked. 'As Caeiro, by sheer unlooked-for inspiration, without knowing or working out what I am going to write. As Ricardo Reis, after abstract deliberation which suddenly becomes concrete in an ode. As Campos, when I feel a sudden urge to write, and don't know what to write about.' This statement, it may be felt, does not really tell us very much. But he adds 'I find make-believe easier and more spontaneous in verse', and these words are particularly significant, because the impression one has on reading the heteronymic poems is that they are convincing enough in themselves, and are hardly made more so by some of the almost gratuitous information Pessoa has provided about the 'characters', and the equally gratuitous attempt to relate them to each other in a master-and-disciple relationship, since this relationship will be found to account for little or nothing in their respective poems. It is above all this dogmatic elaboration, outside the verse itself, which has led critics to suppose that Pessoa was deliberately mystifying his readers. It is one thing to explore different aspects of one's personality, and indeed aspects of the personalities of others (taking literally Pessoa's assertion that at least *some* of the ideas and feelings he expressed were not his own): it is another thing—perhaps an ingenious refinement, perhaps merely a gratuitous complication—to try to relate them to each other in detail, outside the framework of the poems themselves. It is possible that Pessoa was trying to stress, or indeed overstress, that he was not to be identified with his heteronyms, and thus deliberately did all he could to distract the reader from any such interpretation of the poems. He took the risk, of course, that the public might read merely the poems, and not the biographies and other details. We must remember, too, that Pessoa said all this in reply to questions which had been put to him, and by someone who was not a close friend: in other words, it was not a spontaneous confidence. For this reason, perhaps, it is tempting to attach more weight to what he said to Cortes-Rodrigues in 1915 than to what he said to Casais Monteiro in 1935. Yet there are points of contact between the two explanations; they are not mutually exclusive. We have seen that he used the analogy of the dramatist in claiming the right to create characters who were not himself, and that he maintained that his heteronymic work was written dramatically. He returned briefly to this theme in a second letter to Casais Monteiro, dated a week after the first (i.e. 20 January 1935): 'Behind the involuntary masks of the poet, the thinker and whatever else, I am essentially a *dramatist*.'[27]

One more text must be quoted, in which Pessoa himself explained very clearly the difference between pseudonymity and heteronymity, as he saw it. In an article which he published anonymously in the review *Presença* in 1928,[28] he gave the following definition: 'A pseudonymic work is, except for the name with which it is signed, the work of an author writing as himself; a heteronymic work is by an author writing outside his own personality: it is the work of a complete individuality made up by him, just as the utterances of some character in a drama of his would be. The heteronymic works of Fernando Pessoa, so far, are represented by three people, Alberto Caeiro, Ricardo Reis and Álvaro de Campos. These individualities must be considered distinct from that of their author.'[29] If in one sense it is impossible for an author to write 'outside his own personality', it is generally agreed that authors have, from time to time, succeeded in imagining, or creating artistically, characters quite unlike themselves. Whether the result is a masterpiece or not depends to a considerable extent on the degree of empathy of which the novelist or dramatist is capable. At all events, it is interesting to find Pessoa stressing once more the analogy of drama. Indeed, he seems to have made this analogy his chief justification for bringing the heteronyms together in a teacher-and-pupil or poet-and-critic relationship, and for involving them, if not in dramatic conflict, at least in artificially contrived polemics. This pseudo-dramatic framework for the heteronymic poetry is to be seen above all in prose articles of which only a few were published during Pessoa's lifetime.[30] The fact is that there is no real drama: there is merely a static, situational relationship; a *dramatis personae* and an exposition of sorts, but no peripeteia and certainly no *dénouement*.[31]

When Pessoa, towards the end of his life, was classifying his poems with a view to publishing them collectively, he recalled the title of an early group of poems, 'Fictions in the Interlude', and resolved to use the title again, as an overall designation for his heteronymic poetry. This wish of his has been respected in the Brazilian edition of his poetic works.

It is now appropriate for us to consider the three het-
eronyms one at a time, in order to see what their individual
contribution is, in the context of Pessoa's thought and poetic
achievement.

ALBERTO CAEIRO. Caeiro's poetic work, entitled simply
Poemas, is far from voluminous—a mere eighty well-spaced
pages of the Ática edition. The earliest poems attributed to
him were written on 8 March 1914, and the last is dated 10
July 1930.[32] Most were written between 1914 and 1920, six
were written in 1930, and a further three are undated. Forty-
nine poems go to make up 'The Keeper of Flocks', and
another thirty-eight are entitled 'Sporadic Poems'. With
very few exceptions, the poems are in *vers libre*, and there
is no difference of substance between the two groups, the
associations of the first group with tending flocks being
tenuous in the extreme. Indeed, the very first poem begins 'I
have never tended flocks'. It is possible that the idea for the
title was suggested by a poem entitled 'The Shepherdess' by
Alice Meynell, published in 1896. The first verse of this poem
contains the line 'Her flocks are thoughts. She keeps them
white', and in the ninth poem of 'The Keeper of Flocks' we
find 'I am a keeper of flocks./The flock is my thoughts . . .'
But the reminiscence of 'The Shepherdess', if indeed it is a
reminiscence, certainly ends there: Caeiro has no use for the
mysticism of Mrs Meynell.

The recurrent themes to be found in nearly all Caeiro's
poems are wide-eyed child-like wonder at the infinite variety
of Nature, a kind of sensual pantheism, and a calm acceptance
of the world as it is. Caeiro lives very simply in the country
with an elderly aunt. He contemplates the reality of the world
around him and tries to convey in words the innocence, one
might almost say the nakedness of his vision. The emphasis is
in fact on the *manner* of his seeing, not the objects of his
vision. His approach is intellectual rather than descriptive:
the thinker supplants the poet. His language is appropriately
simple, though somewhat abstract, and this in spite of many
familiar expressions. He does not describe particular objects:
he enumerates them briefly, and speaks of them in the most
general terms—trees, stones, plants, seldom anything more

specific than that. Fundamental to his world-view is the idea that in the world around us, all is surface: things are precisely what they seem, there is no hidden meaning anywhere. 'I see absence of meaning in all things',[33] he writes, and Álvaro de Campos relates how Caeiro approved of Wordsworth's lines when Campos translated them for him:

'A primrose by the river's brim
A yellow primrose was to him
And it was nothing more'.[34]

To think about things is simply not to understand them. Our eyes tell us things are different: our thoughts, if we misguidedly allow them to, soon establish irrelevant affinities and begin to classify things. Things simply exist, and we have no right to credit them with more than that. Holding such views, he naturally has no use for metaphysicians or for the sort of poet who suggests that flowers feel, that stones have souls, or that rivers experience ecstasy in the moonlight.[35] We should always see things as though we were seeing them for the first time;[36] otherwise, all kinds of extraneous considerations intervene between us and the object. There is no context: there are only details. There is no whole: there are only parts.[37] The past has no validity, thus memory has no validity either:

'For the Nature of yesterday is not Nature.
What was is nothing; remembering means not seeing'.[38]

It is man who credits things with an inside as well as an outside, and it is man who distinguishes before from after. The allegedly different faces of Nature are not a reality at all: it is we who look at them in different ways. All created things are equal in that they exist equally.

It goes without saying that it is not to Caeiro that we must look for a programme of social reform. 'Let them be like me: they won't suffer then', is all he has to say on the subject.[39] He accepts the existence of injustice as he accepts that of death. According to him, our unhappiness springs from our unwillingness to limit our horizons. We always want to know *whether the sky is blue somewhere else*. If we can only bring ourselves to grasp his simple philosophy, we shall have a basis for unclouded happiness. What man urgently needs is a course of what Caeiro calls *a aprendizagem de desaprender* or 'learning how to unlearn'.[40]

Some of Caeiro's ideas strikingly anticipate certain aspects of

modern existentialist thought: he would certainly have sub-
scribed to what Sartre was later to write in one of the first
pages of *L'Être et le néant:* 'La pensée moderne a réalisé un
progrès considérable en réduisant l'existant à la série des
apparitions qui le manifestent. . . . Les apparitions qui mani-
festent l'existant ne sont ni intérieures ni extérieures: elles se
valent toutes, elles renvoient toutes à d'autres apparitions, et
aucune d'elles n'est privilégiée. . . . Le dualisme de l'être et du
paraître ne saurait plus trouver droit de citoyen en philoso-
phie'.[41] [Modern thought has taken a major step forward
by reducing the existent to the series of appearances which
manifest it. . . . The appearances which manifest the existent
are neither inward nor outward; they are all equal, they all
refer to other appearances, and none of them has any special
privilege. . . . The dualism of being and appearance is no
longer entitled to any legal status in philosophy.] Caeiro
claims to have made this his way of life.

In reality, however, we cannot, as human beings, keep the
element of myth out of our attitudes towards our environ-
ment. We are not just spectators, as Caeiro appears to be: we
have a part to play, we are *involved.* Caeiro will have none of
this. In his glorification of immanence and his dismissal of
transcendence, he is really asking *homo sapiens* to give up
being *homo sapiens.* There is a weakness, too, in his equation
of death and injustice. There are no doubt many forms of 'in-
justice', e.g. floods, earthquakes etc, which in the present
state of knowledge man is powerless to prevent. But there
are many forms of injustice which can be remedied with a
little effort, and the inevitability of death hardly seems to be
a valid argument against social reform. Perhaps this is why
the would-be social reformer in Caeiro's poetry appears in
such an unfavourable light.[42] Pessoa was far too intelligent
a man not to see the bankruptcy of the point of view he
expresses through Caeiro. It is perhaps reasonable to suppose
that in creating Caeiro he was following through, experi-
mentally and systematically, a particular train of thought,
perhaps even a piece of wishful thinking of the type 'How
simple and enjoyable life would be *if only* the human mind
were not made the way it is!' Pessoa, harassed by doubt, con-
stantly frustrated in his quest for metaphysical certainty, and
well aware that analysing things too closely does not make

for happiness, seems to have created in Caeiro a man who thought he had found the answer, and who, by clinging single-mindedly to a limited and blinkered kind of certainty, attained happiness. There is a strangely feverish, over-hearty quality about Caeiro, as though he desperately needed to convince himself that there is no more to things than their appearance, and that he therefore has nothing at all to worry about. But the doctrine he preaches is a superhuman one, impossible of fulfilment for ordinary mortals.

As a reminder of the kind of thing which Caeiro utterly rejects, Pessoa also attributed to him, in the middle of 'The Keeper of Flocks', four poems of a quite different kind, which show us Caeiro actually wishing he were something else, calling plants his brothers and sisters, and saying that the moonlight on the grass reminds him of the fairy stories his old nurse used to tell him. In these four poems, in short, he behaves like the worst sort of sentimental poet, but he himself explains this aberration by saying, in yet another poem, that he was ill when he wrote them, and that the unhealthy ideas he expressed in them indicate the seriousness of his illness![43]

It may be because Pessoa, having tried the experiment, found Caeiro's position untenable, that he killed him off at the early age of twenty-six and, after 1920, attributed very few poems to him.

RICARDO REIS. Though, as we have seen, Pessoa had a vague intimation of Ricardo Reis 'around 1912', this heteronym really dates from 12 June 1914. The last poem dates from 13 November 1935, little more than a fortnight before the poet's death. When we survey the distribution of the heteronymic poems over the intervening years, we find that Reis is the most regular contributor of the three, though there are no poems dated 1922 or 1924, and his total output, in terms of pages, is slight. He is described as 'taught Latin by others: half-taught Greek by himself', and this approximately describes Pessoa's own case. Reis, like Campos, is presented as a disciple of Caeiro, and there are some slight affinities, but they are outweighed by major differences of inspiration and even more of form. He stands, above all, for complete and utter equanimity in the presence of the unknown and the unknowable. He is like Caeiro in urging calm acceptance of the existing order, like Caeiro in the idea of self-limitation, and like Caeiro in that he too is a poet of the country-side, though he has no more interest than Caeiro in the merely picturesque. He is presented as a heathen for whom the gods of antiquity are still real enough, though he suspects that their power is severely limited, since they must be subject, like all things, to Fate. If Caeiro is a pantheist of sorts, Reis is a fatalist. His attitude to Christianity is hostile, because it is an exclusive religion. He believes in Christ, but no more and no less than in all the other gods. The most he will concede is that Christ brought to the old Pantheon a beauty of a kind which was lacking before: an aesthetic attitude, not a spiritual one.[44] For him, the world is unknowable; nothing has any meaning (an obvious point of contact with Caeiro); we are *unaware*, but our very unawareness can be made a source of limited happiness. It is better not to know. Freedom is the illusion of being free, happiness the illusion of being happy; it is better to hope than to possess. The truth cannot be known, perhaps even to the gods. Reis is a striking—and of course artificial—example of the domination of feeling by the intellect. He deliberately cultivates a philosophy which enables him to come to uneasy terms with the immutable forces that govern the world. He tries to cheat, intellectually, by making his desires conform to what little is available to him, and by living out his destiny within the narrow limits of the illusory freedom afforded him. He is a rather melancholy figure, saddened by the impermanence of all things, and by the inevitability of old age and death. The very pleasure he seeks is tinged with sadness, because he knows it is only relative, and that it cannot last. His deepest conviction is of the omnipotence of Fate: he is less convinced of the power of the gods, and at times is even moved to question their reality. *If they exist*, they can only despise us; *if they exist*, it can be for no other purpose than to reward us or punish us. Yet in more sceptical and gloomy moments Reis flatly denies that what befalls us is a reward or a punishment: we have no right to call it anything but an event. It is certain that the gods do not reveal the truth, and it is quite possible that they do not know it themselves. We are all dying, and the end may come at any moment. We must courageously face these facts in full knowledge of them, for mere ignorance is a cowardly state in which to live, and one which affords us no opportunity for exercising our stoicism. The wise man wins inner freedom by severe self-discipline, by an act of abdication, by voluntary submission to an involuntary fate. The wise man 'enjoys' each moment as if it were to be his last—but it is really a question of calm contentment and acceptance, rather than of active enjoyment. On moral issues, Reis does not take sides. An eloquent comment on this is provided by a remark attributed to him by Álvaro de Campos: 'I hate lies because they are *inaccurate*.'[45]

The *Odes* of Ricardo Reis contain obvious reminiscences of Horace.[46] Reis, like the Latin poet, treats the themes of the fleeting hour, the vanity of earthly goods, the snares of Fortune, the changing seasons, the brevity of human existence, life in the country, and even *aurea mediocritas* of a sort. In both, appeals are made to fictitious women bearing such names as Lydia, Chloe or Neæra, though for Reis these women have little or nothing to do with love, and serve above all as a pretext for dialogue or apostrophe. Indeed, for Reis, quiet companionship is preferable to love, because when it comes to an end, as it must, there is less suffering. There are no traces in Reis of the more libertine Horace.

The form in which Reis expresses himself is invariably the ode in *vers libre*, a medium in which he chooses to be brief to the point of being epigrammatic. His dense, intricate, and highly polished style enables him to express the most profound concepts with elliptical concision. His language is conspicuously more abstract than that of Horace: the concrete impinges only rarely. Yet he does not neglect such basic poetic devices as alliteration, well attested, it must be said, in Latin.[47] Indeed, he has deliberately sought to imitate Latin in Portuguese, and has surely gone as far in this as is possible within the bounds of intelligibility. The word-order, in particular, goes far beyond the conventional poetic inversions of Portuguese. He frequently echoes Latin phrases, and occasionally coins from Latin a word not existing in Portuguese, e.g. *proco*, from *procus*, 'suitor'.[48] Not for nothing did Pessoa once say of Reis, with his usual detachment: 'He writes better than I do, but with a purism which I consider excessive.'[49]

It would be no exaggeration to say that in order to appreciate the odes of Ricardo Reis, the reader needs to know at least *some* Latin, and to be familiar with the elements of classical mythology.

ÁLVARO DE CAMPOS. Álvaro de Campos was unquestionably Pessoa's favourite *alter ego*. In verse and prose alike, he contributed, from June 1914 to October 1935, far more than the other two. His poetry, entitled *Poesias*, is almost exclusively in *vers libre*, a notable exception being the early poem *Opiário*, already discussed. It is indeed in his early poems that the influence of other poets, and the preoccupation with current literary theories, can best be discerned. There is something of Mário de Sá-Carneiro to be seen in *Opiário*, written at the last minute for inclusion in the first number of *Orpheu*,[50] and there is a great deal of Walt Whitman in 'Triumphal Ode', 'Maritime Ode', 'Greetings to Walt Whitman', all composed between June 1914 and June 1915, and in 'The Passing of the Hours', written in May 1916. Whitman's influence is apparent in part in the sheer vitality of these poems, in the zest for experience which they express, and in part in the appropriately torrential and exclamatory verse, sprawling in long and irregular lines, and couched moreover in colloquial, everyday language:

'And just as you felt all things, I feel all things, and here we are, hand in hand'

'I'm one of yours, from the feeling in my feet to the sickness in my dreams'[51]

Nevertheless there is in these early poems much that simply corresponds to the spirit of the times, rather than more particularly to Whitman. The spirit of the times, expressed in an extreme form by the futurist movement, called for poetry which would mirror the industrial realities and material preoccupations of the age, and, up to a point, Whitman's preoccupation with matter anticipated this. Whitman showed Pessoa a way of expressing new ideas in verse, and he adopted it, modifying it for his own purposes, and well knowing what its impact would be on a public accustomed to a vastly different poetic tradition. Campos, though far more strident and exclamatory in his early poems than Whitman himself, was on the other hand less enumerative, less sensual, less hearty, and far more thoughtful. Yet there was more than enough, in the poems of Pessoa's Whitmanesque phase, to shock and startle the Lisbon public.

By 1917, Pessoa was already tired of futurism[52] and its ethic of dynamism and even of violence, and had come to realize that he had much to say that would have occurred neither to Whitman nor to Marinetti. He later explained the early Campos poems as illustrating Campos's manner *before* he came under the influence of Alberto Caeiro, whose loyal disciple he then became. This looks like a convenient way of accounting for the abandonment both of Whitman and of futurism. If we compare the typical manner of Caeiro with that of Campos, we can quite imagine that such a poet could have had a general restraining influence on Campos, but we cannot go much further than that, for Campos in the post-Whitman phase, i.e. Campos in the great majority of his poems, is still almost as unlike Caeiro as he was before.

Yet although the first rapture—or excess—wore off, Campos continues to be, as we are reminded from time to time, an engineer and draftsman who has travelled widely and who lives in a big city. In these respects alone he is already very different from Caeiro, and from Reis too for that matter, for though Reis is by profession a doctor, this is something which in no way impinges on his poetry. Campos is far more convincing as a human being, because he is the most in touch with life, and is the furthest of the three from an abstract conception, from the personification of an idea. Even during the Whitman phase, there had been signs of depression in Campos, signs of discontent with himself and with others. Now he becomes *par excellence* the poet appalled by the emptiness of his own existence, lethargic, lacking in will-power, seeking inspiration, or at all events finding it, in semi-conscious states, in the twilight world between waking and sleeping, in dreams and in drunkenness. Reality is impatiently shrugged aside, but keeps returning; dreams are recognized for what they are, but keep impinging. Campos's poetry develops into a kind of sustained polemic between the life of the mind on the one hand, and everyday banality on the other. Which is real? At times he feels that he is a mere spectator: at others he feels inescapably involved. We soon realize that here is anything but a glorification of the modern world or of scientific progress. The prevailing tone is one of agonized doubt, the doubt of a man who feels that he is being dehumanized by his surroundings and is gradually losing his self-awareness. *Taedium vitae*, the painful sensation of leading an absurd and cabbage-like existence, is another important theme. The poet deeply feels all the contradictions in the world around him. The obsessive urge to experience all things—prominent during the Whitman phase—has become an equally obsessive urge to question them. Life seems to be a meaningless jumble of unconnected phenomena, yet surely it cannot be only that: there must surely be some deeper meaning, if only one could discover it. His instinct warns him that the discovery may prove too much for him, but his restless intellect drives him on: he must speculate, investigate, test and probe. Somehow or other he must find out, while doubting in advance the validity of what he may discover. This attitude is diametrically opposed to Caeiro's firm refusal to enquire, based on an unshakable conviction that there is nothing to enquire about. Paradox, graphically expressed, is commonplace in the poetry of Campos, as he sets reality over against imagination, or turns conventional thought-processes upside-down and inside-out.

The style is as far removed from that of Reis as could be imagined, and, though it shares with that of Caeiro a certain colloquial flavour, it is a very long way from Caeiro's calm simplicity. There is an insistent, repetitive, rhetorical quality about it, ramming home the argument and often expressing a growing despair as the poet realizes that the avenues he is exploring are leading him precisely nowhere, or that he is caught in a vicious circle. An atmosphere of unreality is created by insistence on denial, negativity, absence, loss, and removal; a concrete noun, apparently conventionally used at first, suddenly slides over into abstraction. A favourite device is to ring the changes on groups of formally related words *know, known, unknown; conscious, unconscious, consciousness, unconsciousness, consciously, unconsciously*. One has the impression that considerations of form are completely subordinated to intellectual argument, to the need to persuade, or rather to the need to provide overwhelming arguments for doubting whether argument has any validity.

COMMON FEATURES OF THE HETERONYMS. In reality, all three heteronyms were created by Fernando Pessoa. Only in make-believe did they exist independently, and only in make-believe can Alberto Caeiro have 'influenced' the other two. This influence, it must be said, is anything but conspicuous, and furthermore many of the characteristics attributed to the heteronyms in the biographical notes which Pessoa provided have no compelling relevance to what they wrote. One might ask, for instance, just how relevant Reis's monarchist sympathies are to his verse.[53] Or, for that matter, the fact that he is supposed to be a doctor. There is no doubt that Pessoa forged the biographies of the heteronyms after writing at least some of the poems, and though he is at pains to provide them with a different physical appearance, a different education and a different background, the differences thus created have little or nothing to do with the other differences between them, namely the literary and poetic ones.

But what have they in common? In the first place, obviously a creator. One might therefore expect them to reveal, either sporadically or consistently, the preoccupations of their real master. All three are thoughtful, meditative individuals, even Caeiro who claims that thinking is a harmful, destructive process. The poetry of all three conveys to us three ways in which a somewhat abstract superman of the twentieth century reacts to the same dilemma and the same *malaise*. The figures in Nietzsche's *Thus spake Zarathustra* differ from Pessoa's creations only in the degree of abstraction they attain: they are all the mouthpieces of mental attitudes conceived in the abstract, yet Reis, Campos and Caeiro all come to life more than Nietzsche's shadowy figures, though Campos is the most fully drawn character of the three. For all three, the central problem is that of existence itself, and of the reality, or otherwise, of the world. Is there more than one level of reality? Is there more than a surface? Which is the illusion, the outer or the inner reality? The observer or the thing observed? Caeiro tries to regard everything as objective and appears to be successful, at least until he falls ill. Yet it can be said that the transcendental is a major preoccupation of his, since he devotes a great deal of his time and energy to denying that it exists. Ricardo Reis, for his part, doubts whether we can discover anything at all about the world, or about the forces which rule our destinies; but he cannot, like Caeiro, entirely avoid self-torment by simply refusing to speculate. Álvaro de Campos doubts the reality of what he sees, but he also doubts the validity of his own thoughts about the mystery which, he feels, must underlie the world of the senses. Reading the heteronymic poetry—and the same could be said of the ortho-nymic poetry—one becomes aware of an unending and un-equal struggle between the rational powers of man and the life in which he is involved, a struggle in which man is invari-ably the loser. If Campos is the most human of the heteronyms, it is because he is the one who expresses this struggle in the most poignantly human terms.

The critic Mário Sacramento has aptly used the image of the blind alley to describe the world as viewed by these three pseudo-Pessoas. Caeiro considers it pointless to argue whether the alley is a blind one or not, since it is the only *relevant* alley, i.e. the only one available to man. Reis does all he can to forget that the alley must be, can only be a blind one. Campos walks desperately up and down the alley, veering from side to side, and not really expecting to find a way out, but feeling that it would be unworthy of him not to try.[54] So life goes on, meaninglessly, and the heteronyms go on obsessively, wearily, and pointlessly trying to find the answer to the great unanswerable Enigma.

'F.P. HIMSELF'. The heteronyms account for rather more than a third, and rather less than a half, of the Portuguese poems. The orthonymic poetry consists of a large number of items, mostly short and in a variety of more or less conven-tional rhyming patterns, a long Faust fragment, partly in rhyme and partly in blank verse, and, again in various rhym-ing patterns, the collection of poems which he entitled *Mensagem* ('Message')—the only volume of his Portuguese poetry to be published in his lifetime. It will be convenient to consider these three groups in turn. Naturally, there are points of contact with the heteronymic poetry, yet the heteronyms are sufficiently individualized for one to be able to say that *none* of the orthonymic poems as a whole recalls the manner of Reis, of Campos, or of Caeiro. The fact is that, if we were to pay no attention at all to the heteronymic 'labels', and were to read the poems in strict chronological sequence, we would be struck by the amazing diversity, the apparent lack of harmony, and the glaring contradictions in poems dated within a few days of each other. It was perhaps precisely by means of the heteronyms that Pessoa was enabled to sublimate the contradictions he felt in his own mind, and to turn them to a meaningful poetic account. The common feature of nearly all Pessoa's poetry, heteronymic and orthonymic alike, is surely the anguished and unremitting urge to probe the mystery of life. That life is indeed a mystery, and an impenetrable one, is suggested in a great variety of ways, is even denied at times in order the better to affirm it, and yet it is precisely the multiple exploration of this theme which gives Pessoa's work its deep underlying unity.

Is this preoccupation with the mystery of existence, with *Sein* and *Schein*, never absent from his poetry? Rarely. Even the delightful poem he wrote about fairies and children's toys which come to life after dark[55] can be linked with his obsession with the world behind appearances. Most of his orthonymic poetry is enacted at a high and almost ethereal level, above mundane matters, and even above everyday tragedies. The warm human note is rarely present, a notable exception being the deeply moving poem in which he mourns for his closest friend Mário de Sá-Carneiro. Yet even this poem, written eighteen years after Sá-Carneiro's death,[56] is profoundly metaphysical. Campos may have a good deal to say about practical everyday life, though it does not satisfy him, but 'F.P. himself' disregards it most of the time. He may, exceptionally, take some banal incident as his starting-point—a cat playing in the street, for instance—but he soon raises himself and the reader to a more rarified atmosphere, and relates the incident to the problem of fate and of lost identity.[57] Only rarely does he consider an event in purely human terms, as in the well-known *O menino da sua mãe* ('His mother's very own'),[58] but even here, his treatment of the theme, that of a young soldier lying dead on a distant battle-field while at home his mother prays for his safety, can hardly be said to be unrestrainedly sentimental: there are sardonic overtones.

We have in Pessoa, and this is just as apparent in the orthonymic poetry as in the heteronymic, a striking example of the inhibiting power of the intellect on the springs of lyricism. He cannot express feeling directly, because he thinks too much about what he feels, and begins to doubt whether he really feels it, hence his preoccupation with the problem of his own sincerity, a problem vividly treated in the poem *Autopsicografia*,[59] and also neatly summarized in a remark which Pessoa attributed to Álvaro de Campos: 'All true emotion is false at the intellectual level, because that isn't where it happens. All true emotion therefore has a false expression. Expressing oneself means saying what one doesn't feel.'[60] And among his English writings, in a note probably to be dated 1916, we find the following observation: 'Sincerity is the one great artistic crime. Insincerity is the second greatest. The great artist should never have a really fundamental and sincere opinion about life. But that should give him the capacity to feel sincere, nay, to be absolutely sincere about anything for a certain length of time—that length of time, say, which is necessary for a poem to be conceived and written.'[61] This helps to explain the readiness with which he could adopt a particular point of view for the sake of argument, or imagine a reaction not his own, or indeed write a poem 'in the person of someone else'.

The recurring theme, the basic preoccupation of the poetry which Pessoa signed with his own name, is that the world is a terrifying and incongruous place, and that the poet himself is contradictory and absurd. If only we had some means of apprehension *other than our senses*, we would realize at once that the phenomena of the world around us are a mere smoke-screen. We are trapped between the false appearance which is accessible[62] and the reality which is not. We cannot know what lies beyond the appearance. Dreams may provide us with an occasional fleeting glimpse of the Beyond, but we can never recapture this in a waking state. If only we could be conscious and unconscious at the same time! Dreams and memories, memories and dreams, so many barriers between ourselves and the things we contemplate.[63] Certain images recur, suggesting restlessness (the sea), transience (rivers), and mystery (night, fog and darkness). Pessoa's greatest strength as a poet lies in his ability to suggest dream-states, and to create uncertainty (reflecting his own uncertainty) as to the level of consciousness at which something is happening or is being apprehended. Did something happen or not? Was that a distant voice? Was that a footstep he heard behind him? As soon as the poet concentrates his attention, as soon as he begins to listen, or turns round to look, it is as if it had never happened. In other words the interventions of the intellect, often symbolically represented by the senses, have a destructive quality, undermining intuition when the best truths are intuitive. Another important source of strength in his poetry is his skill in suggesting a sense of loss, and of sorrow for what can never be:

'What grieves me is not
What lies within the heart,
But those things of beauty
Which never can be . . .'[64]

We are not far from Julie de Wolmar's conviction that 'le pays des chimères est en ce monde le seul digne d'être habité . . . Il n'y a rien de beau que ce qui n'est pas'.[65] [In this world the realm of fancy is the only land worth living in . . . Only that which does not exist is beautiful.] As for Pessoa's religious attitude, it is well expressed in the poem entitled 'Christmas', which he wrote in December 1922. Gods come and go, and man gets no nearer to the truth: 'Truth/Neither came nor went: Error changed. . . . Neither seek nor believe: all is hidden.'[66]

The fragmentary *Faust*,[67] planned as a drama in five acts, occupied Pessoa intermittently from 1908 to 1933.[68] According to the notes he left, it was meant to represent the struggle between the intellect and life, a struggle in which the intellect is doomed to failure. Each act was to present a different aspect of that failure: Act I, the attempt to understand life; Act II, the attempt to master life; Act III, the attempt to come to terms with it through love; Act IV, the attempt to disrupt it; and Act V, Death, the final defeat of the intellect. That, at any rate, was Pessoa's plan: what he in fact wrote was on slightly different lines, and there are only four headings: The Mystery of the World, The Horror of Knowing, the Failure of Pleasure and Love, and the Fear of Death, this last section being followed by two fragmentary dialogues. The most striking feature of the *Faust* dramatic fragment—apart from the fact that it is totally undramatic—is the intensely personal note, more direct and poignant here than in any of his other poetry, be it heteronymic or orthonymic. It is clear from the outset that the poet identifies himself with Faust, whose preoccupations are precisely his. 'All is symbol and analogy', words uttered on the very first page, may be a reminiscence of Goethe's famous lines,[69] but they are in accordance with Pessoa's thought as expressed elsewhere. Faust speaks of 'this limited and relative world/Through which I drag the cross of thinking as I do'. The world is full of mystery, and 'the secret of seeking is not finding.'[70] 'All the stars, even those which shine/In the unfathomable sky of the inner world,/Are but false trails trodden/By endless steps of error without end.' 'What does existence mean', Faust asks, 'Not ours or the world's—/But *existence in itself*?' When we read the *Faust* fragment after reading Pessoa's other poetry, we have the impression that it is full of quotations, yet on investigation we find that though the point being made is often the same, it is always made in a different way.

Mensagem, published in 1934, is a collection of loosely connected rhyming poems which amount to a symbolist and occultist interpretation of Portuguese history, with a good deal of nostalgia for the past, but also with a strong note of messianic expectancy. To some extent, *Mensagem* (which Pessoa intended to call *Portugal* until just before he published it) is foreshadowed in the intensely patriotic articles the young poet contributed to *A Águia* in 1912, and it is certain that one of the poems dates from 1913. To judge from the dates of the others, it would seem that patriotic themes had preoccupied him as a poet ever since the presidency of Sidónio Pais, May to December 1918. The poems do not *describe* episodes in Portuguese history: the episodes were sufficiently well known to the average Portuguese reader for that to be unnecessary, and in any case it was not like Pessoa to describe when he could evoke or suggest, which is precisely what he does here. He refers indirectly to given incidents or personalities, and extracts a spiritual and mystical significance from them. One poem obliquely recalls the legend according to which Ulysses founded Lisbon (known to the Romans as *Olisipo* or *Ulysipo*); another, the story of Viriathus, the Lusitanian leader who defied the Romans; but the best known ones evoke the wars and voyages of discovery of the fifteenth and sixteenth centuries. *O Mostrengo* ('The Monster')[71] is based on Canto v, stanzas 37–60 of Camoens' *Lusiads*, in which the giant Adamastor, personifying the Cape of Storms, appears to Vasco da Gama and tries, by threats, to make him turn back. The poem *Dom Sebastião*[72] refers to the defeat and death of King Sebastian at Alcázar Kebir in Morocco in 1578. This episode is particularly important in Portuguese history, because it gave rise to legends that the king would one day return. This belief, known as *sebastianismo*, has had many manifestations in Portuguese literature, and it can be said that *Mensagem* as a whole is informed by it. Pessoa's heroes personify the spirit of sacrifice and the sense of a spiritual mission to be fulfilled. Though dissatisfaction, not triumph, is their fate, the poet implies that their restless, questing spirit is as necessary in the twentieth century as it ever was.

The language is abstract and cryptic, the style concise and somewhat elliptical: the poems tend to consist of tightly packed sentences, often without links, even when subordinate or antithetical in sense. One is at times reminded of the style of Ricardo Reis, but with fewer latinisms and a greater syntactical variety.

Mensagem was written—or rather put together, for as we have seen, many of the poems were composed long before 1934—when the Secretariate for National Propaganda offered two prizes for the two best poems on patriotic subjects: five thousand escudos for the best long poem, and one thousand for the best short poem. Pessoa, knowing that his little collection of poems was not long enough to qualify him for the larger prize, submitted *Mensagem* to be considered for the smaller. The prize for the best long poem was awarded to a Franciscan priest, Vasco Reis, for a tedious and absurd attack on Communism, entitled *Romaria* ('Pilgrimage'). Nevertheless, in view of the merit of Pessoa's entry, the prize for the 'second category' was increased to five thousand escudos and awarded to him. To judge from a passage in the long letter he sent to Casais Monteiro in January 1935, Pessoa was not very satisfied with *Mensagem*, because it showed only one side of his personality, and that a secondary one. He felt that he was many things besides a 'mystical nationalist' and a 'rational Sebastianist', and therefore did not attach much importance to this work. Indeed, by January 1935 he was actively engaged in preparing his other poetic works for publication. He was still thus engaged when he died, in November of the same year.

THE ENGLISH POEMS. We have seen that both before he left South Africa and after his return to Portugal, Pessoa wrote numerous poems in English under the name 'Alexander Search'. After 1909 he appears to have abandoned this name, and the English poems which he wrote subsequently all bear his own name. In 1918 he published *35 Sonnets*,[73] which he seems to have composed a few years before. These sonnets were clearly inspired by Shakespeare as to form and verbal intricacy, though not as to content. Though a favourable review appeared in the *Times Literary Supplement*,[74] praising his 'ultra-Shakespearian Shakespearianisms' and his 'Tudor tricks of repetition, involution and antithesis'—certainly conspicuous features of the poems, it must be admitted that they are sometimes rhythmically at fault, and often sound both bookish and constrained. At times he elaborates a conceit and plays variations on it until the mind reels:

> . . . 'Yet joy was joy when it enjoyèd was
> And after-enjoyed when as joy recalled,
> It must have been joy ere its joy did pass' (no. XVI)

Yet in all these poems there is a deep philosophical content, relating, as we have come to expect, to the mystery of life, to death, to reality versus appearance, and a few of them are extraordinarily successful. One of the best, no. XXVIII, is worth quoting in full:

> 'The edge of the green wave whitely doth hiss
> Upon the wetted sand. I look, yet dream.
> Surely reality cannot be this!
> Somehow, somewhere this surely doth but seem!
> The sky, the sea, this great extent disclosed
> Of outward joy, this bulk of life we feel,
> Is not something, but something interposed.
> Only what in this is not this is real.
> If this be to have sense, if to be awake
> Be but to see this bright, great sleep of things,
> For the rarer potion mine own dreams I'll take
> And for truth commune with imaginings,
> Holding a dream too bitter, a too fair curse,
> This common sleep of men, the universe.'[75]

No. V is particularly interesting because it expresses the poet's despair at being distracted by routine tasks from his true poetic mission: 'and I feel beggared of infinity'. In the sixth sonnet, he speaks, as he does elsewhere, of the difficulty he has in feeling emotions, since his intellect always intervenes, destroying spontaneity:

'As a bad orator, badly o'er-book-skilled
Doth overflow his purpose with made heat,
And, like a clock, winds with withoutness willed
What should have been an inner instinct's feat;
Or as a prose-wit, harshly poet turned,
Lacking the subtler music in his measure,
With useless care labours but to be spurned,
Courting in alien speech the Muse's pleasure;
I study how to love or how to hate,
Estranged by consciousness from sentiment. . . .'

The sonnets are, in short, of uneven value. All are concerned with intellectual questions, and are redeemed from triviality and artifice by the high seriousness and even anguish which pervade them.

In the same year, he also published in Lisbon a poem of some 350 lines, entitled *Antinous*, which he had written in January 1915. The probable source for this poem was John Addington Symonds's account, in *Sketches and studies in Italy and Greece*,[76] of a favourite page of the Emperor Hadrian named Antinous, who was accidentally drowned in the Nile during that emperor's expedition to Egypt in A.D. 122 (or 130). Pessoa's poem relates Hadrian's grief for Antinous, and ends with a lament in which the emperor vows that he will have a statue made which shall do justice to the boy's beauty. As regards the nature of their relationship, little is left to the imagination. Pessoa conveys in language of great beauty the utter desolation and emptiness of Hadrian's life in his bereavement. In 1921 the poem appeared again, in a substantially revised form, together with *Epithalamium*, originally composed in 1913, and a third poem entitled *Inscriptions*. These three poems were published by the poet's own publishing-house 'Olisipo'. *Epithalamium*, of about the same length as *Antinous*, may derive its initial idea from a marriage-poem by John Donne, but the bride's mixed feelings about her imminent sexual initiation, merely hinted at in Donne's poem, are lovingly detailed in Pessoa's. The initiation scene itself owes more to Walt Whitman than to Donne, and this is not surprising, considering the year in which Pessoa's poem was composed. Already in 1916, Pessoa described both *Antinous* and *Epithalamium*, then not yet published, as 'most indecent and therefore not publishable in England'. From a letter he wrote in 1930, it is clear that he planned to incorporate the two poems in a larger work which would also contain three more poems on erotic themes: *Prayer to a woman's body*, *Pan-Eros*, and *Antenor*. In Pessoa's view, *Epithalamium* and *Antinous* both savoured of the pagan attitude towards love. The other three poems were to reflect the Christian attitude towards it; but they were never published, and have not been found among his manuscripts. It should be added that the life of instinct, the erotic element, and an ostentatious amoralism, are themes almost entirely lacking in his Portuguese poetry. It may well be that he felt less inhibited, in dealing with erotic subjects, in his second language rather than in his native tongue, but it is also true that he could not have published *Epithalamium* and *Antinous* in Portugal *either*, had he written them in Portuguese. It may not be without interest to note that it was Pessoa who published the extremely out-spoken love-poems of António Botto, Pessoa who translated them into English, and Pessoa who warmly defended Botto when he was attacked.[77] Nevertheless, it can be said that love, when it appears as a theme in Pessoa's Portuguese poetry—which is not often—is highly spiritualized and passionless, a vague communion and togetherness.

The other poem published in 1921, entitled *Inscriptions*, consists of fourteen imagined epitaphs on Greek or Roman tombs. None of these exceeds six lines, and most of them are a mere four lines. They are written in concise and refined neo-classical language which recalls, *mutatis mutandis*, the manner of Ricardo Reis. Here is one of them:

'Me, Chloe, a maid, the mighty fates have given,
  Who was naught to them, to the peopled shades.
  Thus the gods will. My years were but twice seven.
  I am forgotten in my distant glades.'

Naturally, all the *Inscriptions* dwell on the theme of death. The seventh one ends with a line which expresses an idea particu-larly dear to Pessoa, namely that life itself is but a dream: 'Dreaming that I slept not, I slept my dream'.

Two other poems deserve brief mention: *Meantime*, a very short symbolist poem, published in *The Athenaeum* on 30 January

1920; and *Spell*, expressing a yearning for a lost ideal, published in March 1923 in the ninth issue of the review *Contemporânea*.

THE ORIGINALITY OF FERNANDO PESSOA. To his friend Rui Santos, Pessoa once confided that he saw no objection to using the expressions and ideas of others, if they seemed to him to be necessary, or beautiful, or both. We know that he was an omnivorous reader, that he had absorbed what is best in English, French and Portuguese literature, and that he had also read widely in the domains of occultism, theosophy, alchemy, astrology and even magic. He had digested Hegel's philosophy of history, and had found Nietzsche's amoralism, his cult of the superman, and his strictures on Christianity, very much to his taste. He had read Schopenhauer, but it is difficult to assess how far the German philosopher influenced Pessoa, and how far Pessoa found in him ideas which strikingly confirmed his own. For Schopenhauer, the terror of existence is the starting-point for all philosophy, and it is certainly a major preoccupation of Pessoa too. For Pessoa as for Schopenhauer, man is incapable of distinguishing between truth and error, incapable of seeing what lies beyond appearances, incapable of apprehending what Kant had called the *noumenon* or *Ding an sich*, incapable of knowing himself, save as the toy of fate, doomed to frustration and failure, and agonizingly aware of the passing of time. Misery and pain, for Schopenhauer as for Pessoa, are consubstantial with existence itself, hence perhaps the scepticism, particularly of Caeiro but in fact shared by all three heteronyms, about the value of any attempt to reform the world.

Yet Pessoa does not closely follow any one thinker or philosopher. From time to time we may hear an echo or sense an affinity, but it is as though the Portuguese poet, so far as he used other people's ideas or images, deliberately used them in new and startling ways. But what of his *poetic* originality ? As we have seen, there is much of Whitman in some of the early Campos poems, yet Pessoa is clearly far more interested in ideas, and far less exuberantly optimistic, than Whitman was. One of his best-known poems, *Ela canta, pobre ceifeira* ('She sings, poor reaper'),[78] was certainly inspired by Wordsworth's 'The Reaper', and contains verbal reminiscences of it: yet it also contains the typically Pessoan idea of something lacking, and the longing for the impossible. Wordsworth wants to know what the solitary reaper is singing about: for Pessoa, this is a matter of indifference. He wants to be the singer *and yet himself* at the same time. He wants to be, like the reaper, 'blithely unaware', as he puts it, but at the same time *aware that he is blithely unaware*. And the appeal to sky, field and song with which the Portuguese poem ends, is quite lacking in Wordsworth. Caeiro may borrow one idea from Alice Meynell, yet the two poets are poles apart. Pessoa may personally have sympathized with the mystical element in Alice Meynell's verse, but it is anathema to his creation Caeiro. It is possible that the poem 'Night' ('Excerpt from an Ode') was inspired by Shelley's poem 'To the Night', but Pessoa cannot have derived from it any more than the idea of a sustained apostrophe. It may be that the poem 'His mother's very own' owes something to Rimbaud's sonnet *Le dormeur du val*,[79] yet a comparison of the two poems shows that Pessoa's begins at the point where Rimbaud's sonnet ends. Rimbaud provides picturesque details of the spot where the 'sleeper' is lying, but says nothing of his home and family, a major theme in the Portuguese poem. Both poems are extremely effective, but they make their effect in two quite different ways. Valéry, it seems, did not influence Pessoa, yet there are certain affinities between the two. In both, it could be said that the intellect kills spontaneity; both take refuge in abstraction; both are metaphysical minds who rise above the material level; both conceive of poetry as 'the mathematics of feeling'. Pessoa, like Valéry, could have said 'Je me permets de penser qu'il y a de la pauvreté d'esprit à être toujours d'accord avec soi-même'.[80] [I venture to think it is a poor mind that is always in agreement with itself.] And he could have said with M. Teste 'De quoi j'ai souffert le plus ? Peut-être de l'habitude de développer toute ma pensée— d'aller jusqu'au bout en moi'.[81] [From what have I suffered most ? Perhaps from the habit of fully developing my thought —of going all the way in myself.]

What were Pessoa's beliefs ? In a postscript (dated 14 January) to the famous letter to Casais Monteiro of 13 January 1935 (a postscript which Pessoa asked him not to publish) he wrote: 'I believe in the existence of inhabited worlds which are on a higher plane than ours; I believe in the experience of various degrees of spirituality, becoming more rarified until we arrive at a Supreme Being, which presumably created this world' . . . 'I do not believe in direct communication with God, but, according to our degree of spiritual refinement, we shall be able to communicate with progressively higher beings.'[82] The means to this end could be magic, or mysticism, or alchemy, or occultism, and it was above all to the last of these that Pessoa turned as he grew older, for a hankering after the occult *is* a degenerate form of religious feeling—the religion of those who have no religion. For Pessoa, no single church or religion possesses the truth, but they all share in it, because they all assume an expression of the transcendental and a vision of the ineffable. This conviction he once vividly expressed through the mouth of Campos: 'And in every corner of my soul stands an altar to a different god'.[83] For Pessoa, there is what he calls an *Além-Deus*, literally 'Beyond-God', a notion which goes beyond all images and concepts of the divine. He refuses to choose, to commit himself to any one god, for that would mean exchanging the reality for the appearance, the unlimited for the limited, the transcendental for the immanent, the occult for the positive, the soul for the surface. Metaphysical speculation and qualified occultist belief are no mere occasional theme in Pessoa's poetry: they are fundamental to it. Take them away, and there would be little left. Every other kind of subject-matter takes second place, or indeed does not feature at all. This needs to be said, in case it should be thought extraordinary that the eight years he spent in South Africa should have left no trace in his poetry, and even more extraordinary that his everyday life in Lisbon, and that city itself, in which he spent all the rest of his life, should either not appear in his poetry at all, or appear as the vaguest, most shadowy backcloth to the adventures of his soul. A writer of fiction who had never been to Lisbon could describe it more convincingly than Pessoa does. But Pessoa's very nature, and his poetic instinct, prevented him from even attempting to describe contemporary reality at the superficial level. He does not evoke street scenes *à la* Cesário Verde. For him, the superficial level is quite literally that—the surface of things, their least interesting feature, the mere starting-point for speculation about what lies beneath or behind. It was for him as natural as breathing to imagine or believe in the depth and mystery below the surface. Pascal could be terrified by the silence of infinite space: Pessoa is capable of feeling a similar thrill of terror when he contemplates streets and passers-by,[84] or merely the tobacco-shop on the other side of the street.[85] The passers-by are not himself, but they are probably not themselves either, if only they knew it—just masks worn by Someone Else, sheets of paper on which Someone Else writes, pens and ink with which Someone Else writes, a canvas on which Someone Else paints a portrait, mouths uttering what Someone Else says: they do not really live, *they are lived*, by Someone Else. They are happy, because they do not know all this, or even suspect it, and Pessoa envies them, but *he* is doomed to go on thinking and speculating. Bricks and mortar seem inanimate enough, but who knows what reality lies behind the façade—another word for mask. 'Reality', precisely because it has an infinite number of layers, is a thing of excitement and terror for the poet. Each thing suggests its opposite, inescapably: the real—the ideal; material existence —the soul; dreaming—waking; always the same exasperatingly limited Either-Or.

It is not surprising that the image of a *mask* should have suggested itself to Pessoa as a suitable one for conveying the idea of the difference between what seems and what is or may be. He uses it several times, and it is common to his heteronymic and to his orthonymic poetry. And there is more to it than that, for his very name *Pessoa*, meaning 'person' in Portuguese, derives from the Latin *persona*, originally the mask worn by actors, and thus, by extension, 'character' 'part' 'role'. Pessoa certainly knew the origin of the family name, and it is curious indeed that the poet *par excellence* of the quest for lost identity, the poet who is convinced that one reality—or appearance—*masks* another, should have borne such a name. He occasionally played on the modern meaning of his name. *Pessoa* as a common noun is rather more frequently used in Portuguese than 'person' is in English, and some at least of the poet's uses of the word read like deliberate puns.[86]

His poetry expresses the torment of a man who is not content with things as they are, but this has nothing whatever to do with social reform. The things Pessoa is not content with are not the kind of thing which any human agency could alter. Indeed, he has been criticized, with some justification, for a lack of human warmth, a lack of sympathy for ordinary mortals, a lack of interest in their problems. It is rather that he has eyes and ears for only *one* problem, an eternal one which has nothing to do with such temporary accidents as political regimes or social conditions. It is a problem in which all men share to some extent, according to their degree of reflectiveness, or their awareness—usually though not necessarily through religion—of the transcendental. For most of us, however, the preoccupation with the divine or the transcendental is accidental and occasional, not constant or sustained. Most of the time, going about our everyday affairs, we are more like the little-girl-eating-chocolates-and-not-thinking, or the 'unmetaphysical Esteves' of the poem 'Tobacco-shop'. It is the problem of human identity. What is the self? And what is the relation of the self to everything which is not the self? Are we dreaming? How can we tell? What is the relation of the past to the present, in terms of the self? How can we be sure of *anything*, in the last analysis? We are torn between the intuition which believes, and the reason which denies; that is the agonizing dilemma which Pessoa presents so vividly in his verse. So far as man is capable of feeling religious unrest, so far as he is capable of sensing the mysterious element in life and in the universe, so far as he is capable of hungering for the Absolute, so far as he is not content with appearances, so far as he has ever sought and failed to find an overall pattern which makes sense of all its parts, Pessoa expresses our doubts, our fears and our aspirations in a quintessential form. If the intellect is not capable of arriving at the truth, might there not be something to be said for falsehood? For dreams? For fiction? For poetry? If dreams can be a means of cognition, why not fiction and poetry too? But how reliable are dreams? In pessimistic moments he believes the dreamer cannot be right, in optimistic ones he thinks the dreamer is *more likely* (though *never certain*) to be right, while in sceptical moods he simply doubts the validity of dreams. This scepticism can be seen clearly in an English poem which he wrote when he was barely nineteen:

'What is true? What is't that seems—
The lie that's in reality
Or the lie that is in dreams?[87]

Like Baudelaire, Pessoa considers it the role of the poet to *decipher* the baffling signs contained in the deceitful images which parade themselves before our eyes. An intuition that things are complex makes him hostile to any facile or one-sided interpretation of phenomena. The theories of Freud, or the theories of sociological determinism, may explain something, but they are a stimulus to our critical faculties rather than a final answer of absolute validity. This dissatis-faction with *one* explanation helps us to understand why he should have expressed himself in so many contradictory ways, notably, though not exclusively, through the hetero-nyms. At one level, the heteronyms are a mystification: at another, deeper level, they are a serious and profound attempt on Pessoa's part to view things from another angle in an endeavour to understand them or at least to gain some fresh insight into them and into himself. The poet tries to see him-self from the outside, objectively; he is aiming at a kind of utopian abstraction of the self; through simulation, he hopes to find at least a negative definition of himself. *Fingir é conhecer-se*, he once wrote, 'simulation is self-knowledge'.[88] And if poetry is indeed, as T.S. Eliot has suggested, 'not the expression of personality, but an escape from personality',[89] we have a further justification for the heteronyms, if one were needed.

From around 1913 to the end of his life, Pessoa showed a marked preference for the type of poetry in which the subject matter is vague and indefinite, yet lucidly expressed and viewed positively. He cultivates vague, musical qualities in verse, hazy analogues, ambiguous images, deliberately blur-ring the outlines of things and avoiding clear-cut distinctions. His intense and painful awareness of antithesis, of opposites, of the Either-Or, leads him to make frequent use of oxy-morons such as 'a silent cry', 'dark brightness', 'sees blindly', 'the still movement of flowers' and 'far-off anguish . . . near by'. Some of the early poetry, written to demonstrate a theory and to make propaganda points, is extremely obscure and involved, though it contains brilliant flashes, but already in 1914 he was writing some of his best poems, such as 'Oh church bell in my village' and 'Night'; and with the exception of a small number of items of occultist inspiration, his later poetry can hardly be described as obscure, and still less as hermetic. He could be admirably lucid, even when expressing the ineffable and the esoteric. His strength lies in his ability to create a mood, to start a train of thought by suggesting an affinity, a *correspondance* between the material and the non-material world. He intellectualizes feeling, which is another way of saying what he himself makes Álvaro de Campos say: 'All true emotion is false at the intellectual level, because that isn't where it happens. . . . Expressing oneself means saying what one doesn't feel.'[90] It is this idea which he also expresses in two of his English poems: *Feeling,/I thought*—for feeling is unfeatured thought',[91] and 'Thought and feeling's endless schism',[92] and, from one of his best-known Portuguese poems 'What feels in me now is my thought'.[93] When he speaks of anguish and of longing, these 'feelings' are usually to be related to various kinds of intellectual frustration, above all the frustration of being unable to remember, of being unable to re-live earlier experiences, of having to choose between past and present, real and ideal, dreaming and waking. He excels in transposing the vocabularies and the images of emotion and of the intellect.

If there is one fundamental belief which is a presupposition and *sine qua non* of his poetry, it is his belief in the positive value of idealism, in the sense of 'tendency towards the highest conceivable perfection' or 'love for or search after the best and highest', even if some would regard such a quest as madness.[94] He is also the poet of absence, of silence, of nega-tion, for the cause of his sorrow is frequently presented, not as something positive, but as something which is absent, lacking, negated:[95] dreams undreamt, music not heard, things which vanish when you turn to look at them. Even happiness has a negative definition for the poet: it is 'not thinking'. His poetry could be described as confidential, in that it is inspired by real emotions and sensations of his personality, but these emotions are expressed objectively, with reservations as to their validity, or are transmuted and intellectualized. His use of images, metaphors and other figures is anything but conven-tional: it rests on a fundamental principle of occultism, the idea of *correspondances*, and the links are subtle.

What does Pessoa stand for in the poetic tradition? He stands for the denial, not only of sentimentality, but even of sentiment itself as a matter of poetic content. He stands instead for the primacy of thought, intuition, vision and prophecy over sensibility and feeling. His literary ideas, as expressed in a large number of provocative articles, stand in the main for a questioning, a reappraisal, a deepening and heightening of the content of poetry, and for a search for new forms of expression. In his own practice, he introduced into Portuguese a new poetic syntax of the kind already achieved in French symbolist poetry, and he renovated the poetic vocabulary, carefully avoiding, except in parody, anything resembling the stock poetic diction of the accepted Portuguese literary tradition. For many of his contemporaries, this, indeed, and not the content of his verse, was his most remarkable achievement.

He was not a great philosopher, nor indeed any sort of philosopher, but a somewhat unsystematic thinker whose ideas might be termed early existentialist. He is of our time in his *Angst,* in his desperate struggle to make sense of himself and of his surroundings. All his work revolves round the mystery of existence. He has no solution to offer, however, to the problem of the immanence or transcendence of being. Instead, he can only struggle on, dissipating his thought in the complications and contradictions of a mind which feels doomed to absurdity, whatever it does. The only way out is resignation, an acceptance of nausea and tedium as our lot. We can delude ourselves for a while with feigned truths (for since we cannot know the truth, we might as well amuse ourselves by lying and pretending), but *náusea* and *tédio* are always in wait for us, just round the corner. Man comes from one unknown and is on his way towards another. Between him and the universe there is a relationship *of some kind,* but it is unverifiable. What man does, has no value. Obviously, what Pessoa has to say about man and the universe is not constructive: it contains no lessons for living. Man's choice is a limited one. He can shut his eyes to all but appearances, like Caeiro; he can discipline himself to expect nothing, and delude himself that that is happiness, like Ricardo Reis; or he can continue to speculate and go round and round in a vicious circle, like Campos or Pessoa himself, convinced that there must be something there to know, but equally convinced that it is unknowable.

Can we explain the poetry in terms of the man? Or the man in terms of the poetry? Only to a very limited extent, and we would probably be wrong to try. One could imagine from the poetry that he had no aptitude for practical life. His life suggests that he had an aptitude for it, but a limited inclination. The fact remains that, more readily than most of his literary contemporaries in Lisbon, he undertook the practical tasks of editing and publishing, and carried them out with commendable efficiency. In his capacity of commercial correspondent, his advice was often sought in connection with complicated business deals, and it must be remembered that he also edited, with his brother-in-law, a journal of commerce and accountancy, to which he contributed highly technical articles. One would imagine from the poetry that he was a man torn by inner conflict, uncertain of his own identity, and doubting the reality of the world around him, doubting, indeed, even his own reality. And one would be justified. Yet the fact remains that those who knew him in everyday life were unaware of these conflicts and these doubts in him. The clue to this lies probably in his statement to Adolfo Casais Monteiro about his hystero-neurasthenic tendencies: they were purely internal and he did not allow them to manifest themselves outwardly, in his dealings with other people. Pessoa was certainly aware that he was different from other men, that he 'saw' things that others did not see, or want to see, or take seriously, and to that extent, perhaps, we can say that he was 'not understood'. Or rather, in his poetry, he took the risk of not being understood, while in his life he did not, since he suppressed in contact with others those aspects of his personality which made him different, except his astonishing lucidity and intelligence, which he could not easily suppress. At all events, it is always refreshing to find a poet who does not complain that he is misunderstood by his fellow-men, or that he is being victimized by society. What Pessoa finds to complain about is the limitation, the sheer inadequacy of the human mind, primarily, it is true, on his own behalf, but also on ours. He is perfectly aware that the man in the street (or, once again, the little girl eating chocolates) is unconcerned with such problems and is thus far more likely to find happiness than he, Fernando Pessoa, but he accepts this as his destiny, just as he accepted his modest role in society as a commercial correspondent, and refused all offers of greater prosperity.

Not all Pessoa's poetry is of the highest quality, and it

should be pointed out that Pessoa was himself for a long time diffident and fastidious about publishing it. Some of the poems have little substance, or make less effectively a point which has been better made in some of his other poems. Some are probably only rough drafts. Since the poet's preoccupations amount almost to obsessions, there is inevitably an element of repetitiveness in the arguments used, and even in the imagery, e.g. the mask, the well, the empty bucket, the door which is either closed or non-existent. Reis and Caeiro, in particular, make the same limited points over and over again, though of course in different words, different images and different arguments. There is an element of artificiality about the heteronyms, though the worst artificiality lies outside the poetry, in the ill-judged attempt to 'dramatize' their relationship. There is a certain amount of logic-chopping in his way of presenting an argument, but that, again, is more noticeable outside his verse, and is certainly not always meant to be taken seriously. One of his critics, João Mendes, complained that 'his poetic world is like shadows dancing on the wall of a sick-room',[96] the point being presumably that Pessoa allowed his speculations to become a morbid obsession, out of touch with reality. But the same critic admits that for the analysis and presentation of these allegedly morbid preoccupations, Pessoa has no equal.

Above all, Pessoa has the merit of questioning our assumptions, of delving deeper into the things we take for granted, of making us think along new lines, and of presenting things to us in a different and startlingly unconventional way. Many poets have written about suicide, but who ever treated the subject as he has treated it?[97] Many poets have apostrophized Night, but who has done so as Pessoa did?[98] Who ever compared himself with someone else's last look?[99] Who yearned to kiss the harpist's gesture, not her hands?[100] Who has ranged so widely, so originally, so multifariously and at the same time so agonizingly and so poignantly over so many aspects of the mystery of existence and man's quest for identity?

NOTES

1. Published in *Athena* nos. 3 and 4, 1924–5.
2. Published in *Presença* no. 33, October 1931. He had met Crowley when the latter visited Lisbon in September 1930.
3. In *Athena* no. 1, October 1924.
4. According to a draft of the same letter, found among his papers, the other person with the foreign name was 'Captain Thibeaut': see *Páginas íntimas*, p. 101.
5. The prize was seven pounds, to be spent on books. Pessoa chose the complete works of Ben Jonson, *The Lives of the Poets* by Dr Johnson, the poetic works of Tennyson and Keats, and the works of Edgar Allan Poe, with an introduction by Charles Baudelaire.
6. The text of this essay has been reprinted in its entirety by Maria da Encarnação Monteiro in her *Incidências inglesas na poesia de Fernando Pessoa* (Coimbra 1956), pp. 17–22.
7. Ed. Georg Rudolf Lind in *Portugiesische Forschungen der Görresgesellschaft*, Erste Reihe, VI (Münster 1966), pp. 130–63.
8. Like a considerable proportion of his Portuguese poetry, these sonnets were never published in his lifetime. They appeared in print for the first time in the review *Colóquio*, no. 13, April 1961.
9. *Entartung* (Paris 1893–4) 2 vols.
10. Reproduced in *Páginas de estética e de teoria e crítica literárias*, pp. 158–60.
11. The five articles were republished in the journal *Ocidente*, May–September 1941, and again edited by Álvaro Ribeiro (Lisbon: Inquérito, 1944).
12. One is reminded of Arthur Rimbaud's 'JE est *un autre*' (letter to P. Demeny, 15 May 1871). Indeed, the influence of Rimbaud can be seen in some of the early poems of Pessoa, and through him, in the tenets of *paùlismo*. Rimbaud's letter, which has come to be known as *la lettre du Voyant*, was first published in the *Nouvelle Revue française* in October 1912.
13. Re-edited in 1959 by Maria Aliete Galhoz, Edições Ática.
14. In *Portugal*, p. 156.
15. See below, no. 19.

16. Published in *Páginas de doutrina estética*, pp. 24–5.

17. For the full text of this poem, see below, no. 3.

18. Elsewhere, 'Álvaro de Campos' wonders in a poem dated 18 December 1934 whether we are just pens and ink 'with which someone writes — and means — what we set down here'. See *Obras completas* II, p. 65, and also below, no. 31.

19. For the full text, see below, no. 4.

20. Some of the best artistic impressions of Fernando Pessoa are by Almada-Negreiros. The best known is the large painting which hangs in the café 'Irmãos unidos' in the Rossio Square, Lisbon. Almada-Negreiros died in June 1970, aged 77.

21. There may be an echo here of Lautréamont's well-known denunciation of a large number of authors, with opprobrious nicknames. See *Poésies* in *Oeuvres complètes* (Paris: José Corti, 1961), pp. 368–73.

22. *Páginas de doutrina estética*, pp. 27–8.

23. Published for the first time by Maria Aliete Galhoz in the first Aguilar edn. of *Obra poética*, 1960. (2nd edn. (1965), p. 199). Now also published in *Páginas íntimas*, p. 108.

24. *Páginas de doutrina estética* pp. 260 ff. The letter is dated 13 January 1935.

25. The first mention of it occurs in a letter he wrote to two French psychiatrists on 10 June 1919. See *Páginas íntimas*, pp. 69–74.

26. This explains why no one who knew Pessoa regarded him as hysterical or neurasthenic.

27. *Páginas de doutrina estética*, p. 275.

28. 'Tábua bibliográfica', *Presença* no. 17, December 1928.

29. He went on to say 'Whether these three personalities are more or less real than Fernando Pessoa himself, is a metaphysical problem which the latter, not being in the confidence of the gods, and consequently not knowing what reality is, will never be able to solve'!

30. Many hitherto unpublished ones have now appeared in *Páginas íntimas e de auto-interpretação*.

31. If one prefers the analogy with the novel, one could agree with the Mexican poet Octavio Paz that 'Caeiro, Reis and Campos are the heroes of a novel which Pessoa never wrote': see his *Cuadrivio* (Mexico City: Editorial Joaquín Mortiz, 1965), p. 144.

32. In other words, a great many of the poems are 'posthumous', since according to Pessoa, Caeiro died in 1915.

33. From 'Sporadic Poems', in *Obras completas* III, p. 79.

34. For this anecdote see *Presença* no. 30, Jan.–Feb. 1931. Cf. ms. note, in English, dated 1906(?): 'To the rustic a tree is a tree; to a poet it is more than a tree' (*Textos filosóficos* I. p. 120).

35. 'The Keeper of Flocks' no. XXVIII (*Obras completas* III, pp. 51–2). In a document entitled 'Introduction to the study of Metaphysics', possibly written in 1915, Pessoa speaks of the 'spontaneous poetic attitude which attributes feelings to rivers, stones etc', and derives

it from 'a basic anthropomorphism of the human mind' (*Textos filosóficos* I. p. 8).

36. 'Sporadic Poems', in *Obras completas* III, p. 75.

37. Through Caeiro, Pessoa is of course putting his finger on the artificiality, well known to philosophers, of all methods of classification. Cf. Ernst Cassirer: 'All systems of classification are artificial. Nature as such contains individual and diversified phenomena. If we subsume these phenomena under class concepts and general laws, we do not describe facts of nature' (*An Essay on Man*, Yale University Press 1962, p. 209).

38. 'The Keeper of Flocks', no. XLIII (*Obras completas* III, p. 64).

39. Ibid., no. XXXII. See also below, no. 39.

40. Ibid., no. XXIV.

41. Paris: Gallimard, 1947, p. 11.

42. See 'The Keeper of Flocks', no. XXXII, 'Sporadic Poems', p. 77, and below, nos. 39 and 44.

43. 'The Keeper of Flocks', no. XV, introducing nos. XVI–XIX. The text of no. XVI is given as no. 34 below.

44. See in particular *Odes* (*Obras completas* IV), pp. 60–5.

45. See *Páginas de doutrina estética*, pp. 209–10.

46. For a detailed study of this question see Maria Helena da Rocha Pereira, *Reflexos horacianos nas odes de Correia Garção e Fernando Pessoa (Ricardo Reis)* 2nd edn. (Oporto 1958).

47. Note in particular *Odes* (*Obras completas* IV), p. 60 'o fio fiado até ao fim' see below, no. 55, l. 8; p. 142 'vastidão vã que finge de infinito' see below, no. 67, l. 9; and p. 98 'o eco que oco coa'.

48. Ibid., p. 43. See also below, no. 52, l. 25.

49. In the letter to Adolfo Casais Monteiro, dated 13 January 1935, published in *Páginas de doutrina estética*, p. 268.

50. Pessoa describes the circumstances of composition in his letter to Casais Monteiro, 13 January 1935. See *Páginas de doutrina estética*, p. 265.

51. From 'Greetings to Walt Whitman', *Poesias*, pp. 203–4.

52. It is to be noted that it is Álvaro de Campos, not 'F. P. himself', who embraces at least provisionally the cause of futurism, and it is Álvaro de Campos too who expresses enthusiasm for Whitman.

53. It is worth noting, however, that the word *reis* means 'kings' in Portuguese. Perhaps Pessoa meant to imply that because of his name, Reis felt a particular loyalty to the monarchy.

54. Mário Sacramento, *Fernando Pessoa, poeta da hora absurda*, p. 153.

55. *Poesias inéditas* (*Obras completas* VII), pp. 106–7.

56. Ibid., pp. 184–6.

57. *Poesias* (*Obras completas* I), p. 133.

58. Ibid. 219–20. See also no. 9 below.

59. Ibid. 237. See also no. 11 below.

60. See *Presença* no. 5, June 1927, p. 3 (republished in *Páginas de doutrina estética*, p. 168). Cf. *Textos filosóficos* II. p. 99 (ms. fragment, possibly dated 1915): 'Only when it reaches the intellect is feeling expressed. It is of the nature of feeling not to be expressed'.

61. *Páginas íntimas e de auto-interpretação*, p. 210.

62. Caeiro alone accepts this as the ultimate reality.

63. Elsewhere, Pessoa suggests that this difficulty is peculiar to *him*: see MS note possibly dated 1915: 'Between me and the world there is a fog which prevents me from seeing things as they really are—as they are for others. I regret this' (*Páginas íntimas*, p. 27).

64. *Poesias* (*Obras completas* I), p. 170. See also below, no. 13.

65. Rousseau, *La Nouvelle Héloïse*, Book VI, viii.

66. *Poesias* (*Obras completas* I), p. 218. See also below, no. 7.

67. *Poemas dramáticos* (*Obras completas* VI), pp. 75–145.

68. See article by A. E. Beau, 'Über die Bruchstücke zu einem Faust des portugiesischen Dichters Fernando Pessoa', *Goethe. Neue Folge des Jahrbuchs der Goethe-Gesellschaft* 17 (1955), pp. 169–84.

69. *Faust*, part II, act V, final chorus: 'Alles Vergängliche/Ist nur ein Gleichnis'.

70. One may compare this with two lines from no. XXXIII of the *35 Sonnets*: 'And he that seeks, though he on nothing chance,/May still by words be said to find a lack...' A similar idea is expressed in a typewritten note dated 1914 or 1915, see *Textos filosóficos* I, p. 228.

71. This poem has been admirably translated by Jean Longland in Américo da Costa Ramalho's *Portuguese Essays* (Lisbon: Secretariado Nacional da Informação, 1963), pp. 67–8.

72. *Mensagem* (*Obras completas* V), p. 42. See also below, no. 17.

73. Lisbon, Monteiro & Co. The *35 Sonnets* and the other English poems discussed in this section have been included by Maria Aliete Galhoz in the Aguilar edn. of Pessoa's poetic works (1st edn. 1960, 2nd edn. 1965).

74. 19 September 1918, p. 443.

75. This sonnet and several others have been translated into Portuguese by Adolfo Casais Monteiro and Jorge de Sena, and published by Clube de poesia de São Paulo, 1954.

76. London 1898, 3rd series, pp. 184–229.

77. Botto's *Canções* ('Songs') were published by 'Olisipo' in May 1922. The defence of Botto by Fernando Pessoa appeared in *Contemporânea*, no. 3, September 1922. In the following year, Pessoa also defended the poet Raul Leal, who had been attacked by a student organization for defending Botto.

78. *Poesias* (*Obras completas* I), pp. 110–11. See also below, no. 2.

79. Ibid. pp. 219–20. See also below, no. 9. According to Carlos Queiroz (*Homenagem a Fernando Pessoa* Edições Presença 1936, pp. 16–17), Pessoa told him that his poem was in fact inspired by a lithograph he once saw in a *pension* where he dined with a friend.

80. 'Lettre-préface de Paul Valéry' in Père Emile Rideau's *Introduction à la pensée de Paul Valéry* (Paris: Desclée de Brouwer, 1944).

81. Valéry, *Monsieur Teste* (Paris: Gallimard, 1929), p. 137.

82. Quoted in J. Gaspar Simões's biography of Pessoa (see bibliography) II, pp. 232–3.

83. Campos, *Poesias* (*Obras completas* II), p. 221. Cf. 'Polytheism is the

only religion which can be justified' and 'All religions are false, but they represent a way to the true religion' (*Textos filosóficos* 11, p. 63 and 88.)

84. Ibid., in particular 'Demogorgon', pp. 262-3, and below, no. 24.

85. Ibid., 'Tabacaria', pp. 250-7, and below, no. 23.

86. See, in addition to l.19 of no. 20 below, Campos, *Poesias* (*Obras completas* 11) p. 161 'enfolds me like the memory of another *person*, mysteriously mine'; p. 271 'the opium of being a different *person*'; p. 312 'How idyllic life would be, if it were lived by another *person*'; and *Poesias inéditas* (*Obras completas* VIII) p. 168 'I break my soul into pieces, and into different *persons*.'

87. Ed. G. R. Lind in *Portugiesische Forschungen der Görresgesellschaft*, Erste Reihe, VI (Münster 1966), p. 156.

88. Attributed to Álvaro de Campos in *Presença* no. 5, 4 June 1927; now also in *Páginas de doutrina estética*, p. 169.

89. *Selected essays* (London: Faber & Faber, 1932), p. 21.

90. Quoted in full above, p. 40. See also note 60 above.

91. *Portugiesische Forschungen*, 'The old castle', dated 1904, pp. 156-7.

92. Ibid., 'Epitaph', dated July 1907, p. 162.

93. From 'Ela canta, pobre ceifeira', *Poesias* (*Obras completas* 1), pp. 110-11 and below, no. 2.

94. See in particular the poem 'Dom Sebastião' in *Mensagem* (*Obras completas* V), p. 42 and below, no. 17.

95. There is a point of contact with Mallarmé here: see Thibaudet, *La poésie de Stéphane Mallarmé*, 8e édn. (Paris: Gallimard) 1926, p. 136: '(Il) voit dans l'absence la somme des présences idéales, évoquées, pensées grâce au fait même qu'extérieurement elles ne sont pas'. [Absence is for him the sum of ideal presences which are evoked and thought precisely because they have no outward existence.]

96. In *Brotéria*, XLVII, Fasc. 4 (1948), p. 330.

97. Campos, *Poesias* (*Obras completas* 11), pp. 20-3. See below, no. 22.

98. Ibid., pp. 153-7. See below no. 19, and also *Poesias*, pp. 218-19.

99. Fernando Pessoa, *Poesias* (*Obras completas* 1), pp. 45-6. See below, no. 3.

100. Ibid., pp. 41-2.

Fernando Pessoa (*1888-1935*)

He was a thing that God had wrought
And to the sin of having lived
He joined the crime of having thought.

'Alexander Search', July 1907

1) Ó sino da minha aldeia,
     Dolente na tarde calma,
     Cada tua badalada
     Soa dentro da minha alma.

     E é tão lento o teu soar,   5
     Tão como triste da vida,
     Que já a primeira pancada
     Tem o som de repetida.

     Por mais que me tanjas perto
     Quando passo, sempre errante,   10
     És para mim como um sonho,
     Soas-me na alma distante.

     A cada pancada tua,
     Vibrante no céu aberto,
     Sinto mais longe o passado,   15
     Sinto a saudade mais perto.

2) Ela canta, pobre ceifeira,
     Julgando-se feliz talvez;
     Canta, e ceifa, e a sua voz, cheia
     De alegre e anónima viuvez,

     Ondula como um canto de ave   5
     No ar limpo como um limiar,
     E há curvas no enredo suave
     Do som que ela tem a cantar.

     Ouvi-la alegra e entristece,
     Na sua voz há o campo e a lida,   10
     E canta como se tivesse
     Mais razões p'ra cantar que a vida.

     Ah, canta, canta sem razão!
     O que em mim sente 'stá pensando.
     Derrama no meu coração   15
     A tua incerta voz ondeando!

     Ah, poder ser tu, sendo eu!
     Ter a tua alegre inconsciência,
     E a consciência disso! Ó céu!
     Ó campo! Ó canção! A ciência   *over*   20

1)   Oh church bell in my village,
      Plaintive in the evening calm,
      Your tolling ever calls awake
      An echo in my soul.

      So slow and lingering is your rhythm,   5
      So sad, as if on life's account,
      That the first stroke of the sequence
      Has a sound already heard.

      However near to me you ring
      When I pass by, ever wandering,   10
      You seem to me to be a dream,
      In my soul a far-off echo.

      At every sounding stroke of yours
      Throbbing through the cloudless sky,
      I feel the past is further off,   15
      And longing ever nearer.

2)   She sings, poor reaper,
      Perhaps believing she is happy;
      Sings, and reaps, and her voice, full
      Of a nameless joyful loneliness,

      Trills like the song of a bird   5
      In the air clean as a threshold,
      And dips and soars as it follows
      The sweet web of sound her song weaves.

      Hearing her both cheers and saddens;
      In her voice are the fields and hard toil,   10
      And she sings as if she could number
      More reasons for song than life yields.

      Sing then, sing on for no reason!
      What feels in me now is my thought.
      Let the hesitant trills of your voice   15
      Come flooding into my heart!

      Could I but be you, and yet myself,
      Be blithely unaware like you,
      While yet aware of it! O sky!
      O fields! O song! Knowledge is   20

Pesa tanto e a vida é tão breve!
Entrai por mim dentro! Tornai
Minha alma a vossa sombra leve!
Depois, levando-me, passai!

3) *Passos da Cruz.* VI

Venho de longe e trago no perfil,
Em forma nevoenta e afastada,
O perfil de outro ser que desagrada
Ao meu actual recorte humano e vil.

Outrora fui talvez, não Boabdil,   *5*
Mas o seu mero último olhar, da estrada
Dado ao deixado vulto de Granada,
Recorte frio sob o unido anil . . .

Hoje sou a saudade imperial
Do que já na distância de mim vi . . .   *10*
Eu próprio sou aquilo que perdi . . .

E nesta estrada para Desigual
Florem em esguia glória marginal
Os girassóis do império que morri . . .

4) *Passos da Cruz.* XIII

Emissário de um rei desconhecido
Eu cumpro informes instruções de além,
E as bruscas frases que aos meus lábios vêm
Soam-me a um outro e anómalo sentido . . .

Inconscientemente me divido   *5*
Entre mim e a missão que o meu ser tem,
E a glória do meu Rei dá-me o desdém
Por este humano povo entre quem lido . . .

Não sei se existe o Rei que me mandou.
Minha missão será eu a esquecer,   *10*
Meu orgulho o deserto em que em mim estou . . .

Mas há! Eu sinto-me altas tradições
De antes de tempo e espaço e vida e ser . . .
Já viram Deus as minhas sensações . . .

So hard to bear, and life so short!
Pervade my being! Transform
My soul into your fleeting shadow!
Then take me with you, and pass on!

3)   *Stations of the Cross.* VI

I come from afar and bear in my profile,
If only in remote and misty form,
The profile of another being, at variance
With this base and human silhouette now mine.

Perhaps in former times I was, not Boabdil,   5
But merely his last look from the road
At the face of the Granada he was leaving,
A cold silhouette beneath the unbroken blue . . .

What I am now is that imperial longing
For what I once saw of myself in the distance . . .   10
I am myself the loss I suffered . . .

And on this road which leads to Otherness
Bloom in slender wayside glory
The sunflowers of the empire dead in me . . .

4)   *Stations of the Cross.* XIII

Sent as the envoy of an unknown king,
I carry out vague promptings from beyond,
And the sudden phrases which rise to my lips
Suggest to me a sense at variance with their sound.

In unawareness I am torn apart   5
Between myself and my being's mission,
And the glory of my King bids me disdain
This human throng I toil among . . .

The King who sent me, is there such a one?
My mission shall be—to forget why I came;   10
My pride—the desert of self in which I dwell.

And yet! In me I feel sublime traditions
Older than time and space and life and being . . .
My senses have seen the face of God! . . .

5)   Súbita mão de algum fantasma oculto
      Entre as dobras da noite e do meu sono
      Sacode-me e eu acordo, e no abandono
      Da noite não enxergo gesto ou vulto.

      Mas um terror antigo, que insepulto   *5*
      Trago no coração, como de um trono
      Desce e se afirma meu senhor e dono
      Sem ordem, sem meneio e sem insulto.

      E eu sinto a minha vida de repente
      Presa por uma corda de Inconsciente   *10*
      A qualquer mão nocturna que me guia.

      Sinto que sou ninguém salvo uma sombra
      De um vulto que não vejo e que me assombra,
      E em nada existo como a treva fria.

6)   *Abdicação*

      Toma-me, ó noite eterna, nos teus braços
      E chama-me teu filho. Eu sou um rei
      Que voluntàriamente abandonei
      O meu trono de sonhos e cansaços.

      Minha espada, pesada a braços lassos,   *5*
      Em mãos viris e calmas entreguei;
      E meu ceptro e coroa,—eu os deixei
      Na antecâmara, feitos em pedaços.

      Minha cota de malha, tão inútil,
      Minhas esporas, de um tinir tão fútil,   *10*
      Deixei-as pela fria escadaria.

      Despi a realeza, corpo e alma,
      E regressei à noite antiga e calma
      Como a paisagem ao morrer do dia.

7)   *Natal*

      Nasce um deus. Outros morrem. A Verdade
      Nem veio nem se foi: o Erro mudou.
      Temos agora uma outra Eternidade,
      E era sempre melhor o que passou.   *over*

5)   The sudden hand of some mysterious ghost
      Between the folds of night and of my sleep
      Shakes me to wakefulness, and helpless
      In the night I discern neither shape nor movement.

      But an age-old dread, which I bear   *5*
      In my heart unburied, as from a throne
      Descending asserts itself my lord and master
      With no imperious word or nod or insult.

      And all at once I feel my life
      Bound with a bond of Unconsciousness   *10*
      To some nocturnal hand which guides me.

      I feel that I am no one but the shadow
      Of a shape which awes me though I see it not,
      And I exist in nothing, like the chilly dark.

6)   *Abdication*

      Take me in your arms, eternal night,
      And call me your son. I am a king
      Who gave up of his own accord
      His throne of weariness and dreams.

      My sword, a burden to my failing arms,   *5*
      I gave to calm and manly hands to wield;
      My sceptre and crown I left behind
      Smashed to pieces in the antechamber.

      My coat of mail, so useless,
      My spurs so vainly jingling,   *10*
      I left on the grand and chilly stairs.

      Body and soul, I threw off kingship
      And returned to the calm of age-old night,
      As does the landscape at the death of day.

7)   *Christmas*

      A god is born: others die. Truth
      Neither came nor went: Error changed.
      A fresh Eternity has dawned for us:
      What went before was always best.

Cega, a Ciência a inútil gleba lavra.   *5*
Louca, a Fé vive o sonho do seu culto.
Um novo deus é só uma palavra.
Não procures nem creias: tudo é oculto.

8)   *O Andaime*

O tempo que eu hei sonhado
Quantos anos foi de vida!
Ah, quanto do meu passado
Foi só a vida mentida
De um futuro imaginado!   *5*

Aqui à beira do rio
Sossego sem ter razão.
Este seu correr vazio
Figura, anónimo e frio,
A vida vivida em vão.   *10*

A 'sp'rança que pouco alcança!
Que desejo vale o ensejo?
E uma bola de criança
Sobe mais que a minha 'sp'rança.
Rola mais que o meu desejo.   *15*

Ondas do rio, tão leves
Que não sois ondas sequer,
Horas, dias, anos, breves
Passam—verduras ou neves
Que o mesmo sol faz morrer.   *20*

Gastei tudo que não tinha.
Sou mais velho do que sou.
A ilusão, que me mantinha,
Só no palco era rainha:
Despiu-se, e o reino acabou.   *25*

Leve som das águas lentas,
Gulosas da margem ida,
Que lembranças sonolentas
De esperanças nevoentas!
Que sonhos o sonho e a vida!   *over*   *30*

Blindly, Knowledge turns the sterile soil.   5
Madly, Faith lives the dream religion bids.
A new god is the merest word.
Neither seek nor believe: all is hidden.

8)   *Scaffolding*

How many years of life
Were those I dreamed away!
Oh how much of my past
Was but the living lie
Of fancied future days!   5

Here on the bank of the river,
Perversely I am at peace.
This its futile flowing
Stands, cold and nameless symbol,
For life lived in vain.   10

How little hope achieves!
What desire can match the moment?
Even a child's ball
Bounces higher than my hope,
Rolls further than my desire.   15

Waves of the river, so slight
You are not even waves,
Hours, days and years—too brief
Their passing: leaves or snows
Which the same sun consumes.   20

I wasted all I never had.
I am older than my years.
The illusion which sustained me
Was queen, but only on the stage:
When she disrobed, the reign was over.   25

Slight sound of languid waters,
Greedy for the bank now past,
What drowsy memories
Of hazy hopes!
Living or dreaming—both but dreams!   30

Que fiz de mim? Encontrei-me
Quando estava já perdido.
Impaciente deixei-me
Como a um louco que teime
No que lhe foi desmentido.   *35*

Som morto das águas mansas
Que correm por ter que ser,
Leva não só as lembranças,
Mas as mortas esperanças—
Mortas, porque hão-de morrer.   *40*

Sou já o morto futuro.
Só um sonho me liga a mim—
O sonho atrasado e obscuro
Do que eu devera ser—muro
Do meu deserto jardim.   *45*

Ondas passadas, levai-me
Para o olvido do mar!
Ao que não serei legai-me,
Que cerquei com um andaime
A casa por fabricar.   *50*

9) *O Menino da sua Mãe*

No plaino abandonado
Que a morna brisa aquece,
De balas traspassado
—Duas, de lado a lado—,
Jaz morto, e arrefece.   *5*

Raia-lhe a farda o sangue.
De braços estendidos,
Alvo, louro, exangue,
Fita com olhar langue
E cego os céus perdidos.   *10*

Tão jovem! que jovem era!
(Agora que idade tem?)
Filho único, a mãe lhe dera
Um nome e o mantivera:
'O menino da sua mãe'.   *over*   *15*

What became of me? I found myself
As one already lost.
Impatiently I turned away
As from a madman who persists
In saying black is white.   *35*

Dead sound of gentle waters
Flowing because doomed to flow,
Take with you not memories alone,
But dead hopes too—
Dead, for die they must.   *40*

Already I am the future corpse.
A mere dream binds me to myself—
The dim and laggard dream
Of what I should have been—a wall
In my deserted garden.   *45*

Waves now past, come bear me
To the sea's oblivion!
Bind me to what I am not to be,
I who ringed with scaffolding
The house as yet unbuilt.   *50*

9) *His Mother's Very Own*

The warm wind sweeps
The deserted plain.
Pierced by two bullets
Through and through,
He lies there dead and cold.   *5*

Blood streaks his tunic.
With arms outstretched,
Blond, bloodless, ghastly white,
With blind and listless gaze
He stares at the vanished sky.   *10*

He was so young, so very young!
(How old can he be now?)
His mother gave this only son
A name she never changed:
'His mother's very own'.   *15*

Caiu-lhe da algibeira
A cigarreira breve.
Dera-lha a mãe. Está inteira
E boa a cigarreira.
Ele é que já não serve.   20

De outra algibeira, alada
Ponta a roçar o solo,
A brancura embainhada
De um lenço . . . Deu-lho a criada
Velha que o trouxe ao colo.   25

Lá longe, em casa, há a prece:
'Que volte cedo, e bem!'
(Malhas que o Império tece!)
Jaz morto, e apodrece,
O menino da sua mãe.   30

10)   Se sou alegre ou sou triste? . . .
        Francamente, não o sei.
        A tristeza em que consiste?
        Da alegria o que farei?

        Não sou alegre nem triste.   5
        Verdade, não sei que sou.
        Sou qualquer alma que existe
        E sinto o que Deus fadou.

        Afinal, alegre ou triste?
        Pensar nunca tem bom fim . . .   10
        Minha tristeza consiste
        Em não saber bem de mim . . .
        Mas a alegria é assim . . .

11)   *Autopsicografia*

        O poeta é um fingidor.
        Finge tão completamente
        Que chega a fingir que é dor
        A dor que deveras sente.   *over*

From his pocket, all too soon,
The cigarette-case fell—
His mother's gift. The case
Is still as good as new:
He's fit for nothing now.   20

From another pocket droops
Brushing the ground
The white hem of a handkerchief,
The gift of the old servant
Who carried him in her arms.   25

Far away at home the prayer goes up:
'May he soon come back in health!'
(Such is the web that Empire weaves!)
He lies there dead, and soon to rot,
His mother's very own.   30

10) 'Joyful or sad?', you ask of me . . .
I frankly don't know which.
What is sadness anyway?
What use have I for joy?

I'm neither sad nor joyful.   5
I really don't know what I am.
I'm a soul that happens to exist,
And I feel what God ordained.

Which is it, then, joyful or sad?
Thinking does no good at all . . .   10
My sadness is just
My own uncertainty . . .
The same could be said of joy.

11) *Self-Analysis*

The poet's good at pretending,
Such a master of the art
He even manages to pretend
The pain he really feels is pain.

E os que lêem o que escreve,   *5*
Na dor lida sentem bem,
Não as duas que ele teve,
Mas só a que eles não têm.

E assim nas calhas de roda
Gira, a entreter a razão,   *10*
Esse comboio de corda
Que se chama o coração.

12)   *Isto*

Dizem que finjo ou minto
Tudo que escrevo. Não.
Eu simplesmente sinto
Com a imaginação.
Não uso o coração.   *5*

Tudo o que sonho ou passo,
O que me falha ou finda,
É como que um terraço
Sobre outra coisa ainda.
Essa coisa é que é linda.   *10*

Por isso escrevo em meio
Do que não está ao pé,
Livre do meu enleio,
Sério do que não é.
Sentir? Sinta quem lê!   *15*

13)   O que me dói não é
O que há no coração
Mas essas coisas lindas
Que nunca existirão . . .

São as formas sem forma   *5*
Que passam sem que a dor
As possa conhecer
Ou as sonhar o amor.

São como se a tristeza
Fosse árvore e, uma a uma,   *10*
Caíssem suas folhas
Entre o vestígio e a bruma.

And those who read his written words   5
Feel, as they read of pain,
Not the two kinds that were his
But only the kind that's not theirs.

And so around its little track,
To entertain the mind,   10
Runs that clockwork train of ours,
The thing we call the heart.

12)   *This*

They say that all I ever write
Is but pretence and lies. Not so.
It's simply that I feel
With the imagination.
I do without the heart.   5

All I dream or live through,
All I lack, all that falls short,
Is as it were a terrace
With a view of something more—
And *that's* a thing of beauty.   10

So when I write I'm in the midst
Of what is far from me,
Completely uninvolved myself,
In earnest for no reason.
Feelings? They're for the reader!   15

13)   What grieves me is not
What lies within the heart,
But those things of beauty
Which never can be . . .

They are the shapeless shapes   5
Which pass, though sorrow
Cannot know them
Nor love dream them.

They are as though sadness
Were a tree and, one by one,   10
Its leaves were to fall
Half outlined in the mist.

14) Quando era criança
     Vivi, sem saber,
     Só para hoje ter
     Aquela lembrança.

     É hoje que sinto   5
     Aquilo que fui.
     Minha vida flui,
     Feita do que minto.

     Mas nesta prisão,
     Livro único, leio   10
     O sorriso alheio
     De quem fui então.

15) Houve um ritmo no meu sono.
     Quando acordei o perdi.
     Porque saí do abandono
     De mim mesmo, em que vivi?

     Não sei que era o que não era.   5
     Sei que suave me embalou,
     Como se o embalar quisera
     Tornar-me outra vez quem sou.

     Houve uma música finda
     Quando acordei de a sonhar.   10
     Mas não morreu: dura ainda
     No que me faz não pensar.

From MENSAGEM

16) *Mar português*

     Ó mar salgado, quanto do teu sal
     São lágrimas de Portugal!
     Por te cruzarmos, quantas mães choraram,
     Quantos filhos em vão rezaram!
     Quantas noivas ficaram por casar   5
     Para que fosses nosso, ó mar!

over

14)   A child I lived
       Yet never knew
       It was all so that I
       Might remember it now.

       Only now do I feel   *5*
       What then I was.
       My life flows on,
       A compound of my lies.

       But in this prison
       My only book I read: *10*
       The smile of another—
       The one I was then.

15)   There was a rhythm in my sleep.
       When I awoke I lost it.
       Why did I ever cease to live
       That erstwhile self-surrender?

       I know not what it was, that was not.   *5*
       I know it lulled me softly,
       As though the very lulling would
       Make me once more the one I am.

       There was music that was over
       When I awoke from dreaming it.   *10*
       It did not die: it still endures
       In what inhibits thought in me.

16)   *Portuguese Sea*

       Oh salty sea, how much of thee
       Portugal shed as tears!
       Because we crossed thee, how many mothers wept,
       How many sons prayed to no avail!
       How many plighted maids remained unwed   *5*
       That we might possess thee, O sea!

Valeu a pena? Tudo vale a pena
Se a alma não é pequena.
Quem quer passar além do Bojador
Tem que passar além da dor.   *10*
Deus ao mar o perigo e o abismo deu,
Mas nele é que espelhou o céu.

17) *Dom Sebastião, Rei de Portugal*

Louco, sim, louco, porque quis grandeza
Qual a Sorte a não dá.
Não coube em mim minha certeza;
Por isso onde o areal está
Ficou meu ser que houve, não o que há.   *5*

Minha loucura, outros que me a tomem
Com o que nela ia.
Sem a loucura que é o homem
Mais que a besta sadia,
Cadáver adiado que procria?   *10*

18) *As Ilhas Afortunadas*

Que voz vem no som das ondas
Que não é a voz do mar?
É a voz de alguém que nos fala,
Mas que, se escutamos, cala,
Por ter havido escutar.   *5*

E só se, meio dormindo,
Sem saber de ouvir ouvimos,
Que ela nos diz a esperança
A que, como uma criança
Dormente, a dormir sorrimos.   *10*

São ilhas afortunadas,
São terras sem ter lugar,
Onde o Rei mora esperando.
Mas, se vamos despertando,
Cala a voz, e há só o mar.   *15*

Was it worth while? All is worth while
If only the soul be not base.
He who would sail beyond Cape Bojador
Must sail beyond the bourn of grief.   *10*
God gave the sea its dangers and its deeps,
But in it He mirrored heaven's own face.

17) *Dom Sebastian, King of Portugal*

Mad, yes, mad, because I sought a greatness
Not in the gift of Fate.
I could not contain the certainty I felt;
Therefore, on the sandy waste
Remained what my being was, not is.   *5*

Let my madness pass to other men
With all that it implied.
Without madness, what is man
More than the healthy beast,
A postponed and procreating corpse?   *10*

18) *The Islands of the Blest*

What voice that is not the voice of the sea
Comes borne on the sound of the waves?
'Tis the voice of one who speaks to us,
But if we hearken it is still,
Because of the hearkening.   *5*

And only if, half sleeping,
We hear without knowing we hear,
Does it tell us of the hope
At which, like a child
Asleep, we smile in our sleep.   *10*

In islands of the blest
In lands nowhere in space,
There dwells the King who waits.
But if we begin to awake,
The voice is still: there is but the sea.   *15*

END OF *Pessoa*

19)   *Excerto de uma Ode*

Vem, Noite antiquíssima e idêntica,
Noite Rainha nascida destronada,
Noite igual por dentro ao silêncio, Noite
Com as estrelas lantejoulas rápidas
No teu vestido franjado de Infinito.   *5*

Vem, vagamente,
Vem, levemente,
Vem sòzinha, solene, com as mãos caídas
Ao teu lado, vem
E traz os montes longínquos para o pé das árvores próximas,   *10*
Funde num campo teu todos os campos que vejo,
Faze da montanha um bloco só do teu corpo,
Apaga-lhe todas as diferenças que de longe vejo,
Todas as estradas que a sobem,
Todas as várias árvores que a fazem verde-escuro ao longe,   *15*
Todas as casas brancas e com fumo entre as árvores,
E deixa só uma luz e outra luz e mais outra,
Na distância imprecisa e vagamente perturbadora,
Na distância sùbitamente impossível de percorrer.

Nossa Senhora   *20*
Das coisas impossíveis que procuramos em vão,
Dos sonhos que vêm ter connosco ao crepúsculo, à janela,
Dos propósitos que nos acariciam
Nos grandes terraços dos hotéis cosmopolitas
Ao som europeu das músicas e das vozes longe e perto,   *25*
E que doem por sabermos que nunca os realizaremos . . .
Vem, e embala-nos,
Vem e afaga-nos,
Beija-nos silenciosamente na fronte,
Tão levemente na fronte que não saibamos que nos beijam   *30*
Senão por uma diferença na alma,
E um vago soluço partindo melodiosamente
Do antiquíssimo de nós
Onde têm raiz todas essas árvores de maravilha
Cujos frutos são os sonhos que afagamos e amamos   *35*
Porque os sabemos fora de relação com o que há na vida.

over

19)   *Excerpt from an Ode*

Come, age-old never-changing Night,
Night born a queen without a throne,
Night inwardly the same as silence, Night
With starry sequins fleeting
In your robe fringed with the Infinite.   *5*

Come, dimly seen,
Come, lightly felt,
Come in lone majesty, holding your hands
Limp at your sides, come
And bring the far-off hills close to the trees near-by,   *10*
Merge in one field of yours all the fields I see,
Make the mountain one mass with the shape of your body,
Blot out from it all the features I see from afar,
All the roads climbing it,
All the many trees making it dark green far away,   *15*
All the white houses among the trees, and their smoke,
And leave just one light, another light and yet another
In the vague and dimly disturbing distance,
The distance all at once impossible to cross.

Our Lady   *20*
Of the impossible things we seek in vain,—
The dreams which come to us at twilight, by the window,
The plans which caress us
On the wide terraces of cosmopolitan hotels
To the European sound of music and of voices far and near, *25*
And hurt because we know we shall never fulfil them . . .
Come and lull us,
Come and soothe us,
Silently kiss our brows,
Our brows so lightly that we know it is a kiss   *30*
Only by a difference in the soul,
And the hint of a sob melodiously wrung
From what is age-old in us
Where all those wondrous trees have their roots,
Trees whose fruits are the dreams we love and cherish,   *35*
Knowing that they have no link with what there is in life.

Vem soleníssima,
Soleníssima e cheia
De uma oculta vontade de soluçar,
Talvez porque a alma é grande e a vida pequena,   40
E todos os gestos não saem do nosso corpo
E só alcançamos onde o nosso braço chega,
E só vemos até onde chega o nosso olhar.

Vem, dolorosa,
Mater-Dolorosa das Angústias dos Tímidos,   45
Turris-Eburnea das Tristezas dos Desprezados,
Mão fresca sobre a testa em febre dos Humildes,
Sabor de água sobre os lábios secos dos Cansados.
Vem, lá do fundo
Do horizonte lívido,   50
Vem e arranca-me
Do solo de angústia e de inutilidade
Onde vicejo.
Apanha-me do meu solo, malmequer esquecido,
Folha a folha lê em mim não sei que sina   55
E desfolha-me para teu agrado,
Para teu agrado silencioso e fresco.
Uma folha de mim lança para o Norte,
Onde estão as cidades de Hoje que eu tanto amei;
Outra folha de mim lança para o Sul,   60
Onde estão os mares que os Navegadores abriram;
Outra folha de mim atira ao Ocidente,
Onde arde ao rubro tudo o que talvez seja o Futuro,
Que eu sem conhecer adoro;
E a outra, as outras, o resto de mim   65
Atira ao Oriente,
Ao Oriente donde vem tudo, o dia e a fé,
Ao Oriente pomposo e fanático e quente,
Ao Oriente excessivo que eu nunca verei,
Ao Oriente budista, bramânico, sintoísta,   70
Ao Oriente que tudo o que nós não temos,
Que tudo o que nós não somos,
Ao Oriente onde—quem sabe?—Cristo talvez ainda hoje viva,
Onde Deus talvez exista realmente e mandando tudo . . .

over

Come in full majesty,
In full majesty, imbued
With a hidden urge to sob,
Perhaps because the soul is vast and life is paltry,   40
And all our gestures go no further than our bodies,
And we can only reach to where our arms extend,
And we can only see as far as our gaze reaches.

Come in sorrow,
Mater-Dolorosa to the Anguish of the Timid,   45
Turris-Eburnea to the Distress of the Despised,
Cool hand on the fevered brow of the Humble,
Taste of water on the parched lips of the Weary.
Come from the remoteness
Of the wan horizon,   50
Come and pluck me
From the soil of vanity and anguish
Where my growth is rank.
Gather this marigold where it lies forgotten,
Petal by petal read in me some fate I do not know,   55
And for your pleasure strip me of my petals,
For your cool and silent pleasure.
Cast one petal of me to the North,
Where lie today's cities, so dear to me once;
Another petal of me cast to the South,   60
Where lie the seas the Navigators opened;
Another of my petals throw to the West,
Where glows with red heat all that yet may come to pass,
Which I worship though I know it not;
And the other petal, the others, the rest of me   65
Throw to the East,
The East whence come all things, the dawn and faith,
The East of pomp, fanatic zeal, and heat,
The excessive East, which I shall never see,
The East of Buddha, of Brahma and of Shinto,   70
The East—the All that we have not,
The All that we are not,
The East where—who knows?—Christ may still live to this day,
Where God may exist indeed as Lord of all . . .

Vem sobre os mares,   *75*
Sobre os mares maiores,
Sobre os mares sem horizontes precisos,
Vem e passa a mão pelo dorso de fera,
E acalma-o misteriosamente,
Ó domadora hipnótica das coisas que se agitam muito!   *80*

Vem, cuidadosa,
Vem, maternal,
Pé antepé enfermeira antiquíssima, que te sentaste
À cabeceira dos deuses das fés já perdidas,
E que viste nascer Jeová e Júpiter,   *85*
E sorriste porque tudo te é falso e inútil.

Vem, Noite silenciosa e extática,
Vem envolver na noite manto branco
O meu coração . . .
Serenamente como uma brisa na tarde leve,   *90*
Tranquilamente como um gesto materno afagando,
Com as estrelas luzindo nas tuas mãos
E a lua máscara misteriosa sobre a tua face.
Todos os sons soam de outra maneira
Quando tu vens.   *95*
Quando tu entras baixam todas as vozes,
Ninguém te vê entrar.
Ninguém sabe quando entraste,
Senão de repente, vendo que tudo se recolhe,
Que tudo perde as arestas e as cores,   *100*
E que no alto céu ainda claramente azul
Já crescente nítido, ou círculo branco, ou mera luz nova que
    vem,

A lua começa a ser real.

20)   *Lisbon Revisited* (1923)

Não: não quero nada.
Já disse que não quero nada.

Não me venham com conclusões!
A única conclusão é morrer.   *over*

Come over the seas,   *75*
Over the wider seas,
Over the seas unbounded by horizons,
Come, and stroke the wild beast's back,
And calm it mysteriously,
Oh hypnotic tamer of deeply restless things!   *80*

Come, full of care,
Come like a mother,
On tiptoe, age-old nurse who sat
At the bedside of the gods of faiths now vanished,
Who saw the birth of Jehovah and Jupiter,   *85*
And smiled because to you all things are false and vain.

Come, silent and ecstatic Night,
Come, wrap my heart in the pale folds
Of night's cloak . . .
Serenely like a breeze in the gentleness of evening,   *90*
Calmly like a mother's gesture soothing,
With the stars shining in your hands
And the moon's mystery masking your features.
All sounds sound different
At your coming.   *95*
At your entry all voices are lowered,
No one sees you enter.
No one knows when you entered,
Except when suddenly all things are seen to fade,
Losing their outlines and their colours,   *100*
While in the sky above, still clearly blue,
Already a gleaming crescent, or a white disk, or just a new
    light dawning,

The moon begins to be real.

20) *Lisbon Revisited* (1923)

No, there's nothing I want.
I tell you there's nothing I want.

Don't come to me with your conclusions!
Death is the only conclusion there is.

Não me tragam estéticas!   *5*
Não me falem em moral!
Tirem-me daqui a metafísica!
Não me apregoem sistemas completos, não me enfileirem
     conquistas
Das ciências (das ciências, Deus meu, das ciências!)—
Das ciências, das artes, da civilização moderna!   *10*

Que mal fiz eu aos deuses todos?

Se têm a verdade, guardem-a!
Sou um ténico, mas tenho técnica só dentro da técnica.
Fora disso sou doido, com todo o direito a sê-lo.
Com todo o direito a sê-lo, ouviram?   *15*

Não me macem, por amor de Deus!

Queriam-me casado, fútil, quotidiano e tributável?
Queriam-me o contrário disto, o contrário de qualquer coisa?
Se eu fosse outra pessoa, fazia-lhes, a todos, a vontade.
Assim, como sou, tenham paciência!   *20*
Vão para o diabo sem mim,
Ou deixem-me ir sòzinho para o diabo!
Para que havemos de ir juntos?

Não me peguem no braço!
Não gosto que me peguem no braço. Quero ser sòzinho.   *25*
Já disse que sou sòzinho!
Ah, que maçada quererem que eu seja de companhia!
Ó céu azul—o mesmo da minha infância—,
Eterna verdade vazia e perfeita!
Ó macio Tejo ancestral e mudo,   *30*
Pequena verdade onde o céu se reflecte!
Ó mágoa revisitada, Lisboa de outrora de hoje!
Nada me dais, nada me tirais, nada sois que eu me sinta.

Deixem-me em paz! Não tardo, que eu nunca tardo . . .
E enquanto tarda o Abismo e o Silêncio quero estar sòzinho!   *35*

21)   *Lisbon Revisited* (1926)

Nada me prende a nada.
Quero cinquenta coisas ao mesmo tempo.   *over*

Don't give me aesthetic theories!   *5*
Don't talk to me about morality!
Take away your metaphysics!
Don't try to sell me foolproof systems, don't reel off the
   achievements
Of science (science, for God's sake, science!)—
Of science, the arts and modern civilization!   *10*

What harm have I done to all the gods?

If they've got the truth, let them keep it!
I'm a technician, but I'm technical only within my technique.
Apart from that, I'm mad, with every right to be.
Every right to be, do you hear?   *15*

For heaven's sake stop boring me!

You'd like me to be married, humdrum, a tax-paying nobody?
You'd like me to be the opposite, the opposite of something?
If I were someone else, I'd let you all have your way.
You must put up with me just as I am.   *20*
Go to hell without me,
Or let me go to hell on my own!
Why should we go there together?

Don't take my arm!
I don't like having my arm taken. I want to be alone.   *25*
I'm on my own, I tell you!
How boring to be expected to join in!
Oh blue sky—the same as in my childhood—,
Eternal truth, so perfect and so empty!
Oh smooth, mute, ancestral Tagus,   *30*
Particle of truth mirroring the sky!
Oh sorrow visited anew, today's Lisbon of former times!
You give me nothing, you take nothing away, you're nothing I
   can feel.

Leave me in peace! I won't delay, I never do . . .
And as long as the Abyss and Silence delay, I want to stay alone!

21)   *Lisbon Revisited* (1926)

Nothing holds me to anything.
I want fifty things at the same time.

Anseio com uma angústia de fome de carne
O que não sei que seja—
Definidamente pelo indefinido . . .   5
Durmo irrequieto, e vivo num sonhar irrequieto
De quem dorme irrequieto, metade a sonhar.

Fecharam-me todas as portas abstractas e necessárias.
Correram cortinas de todas as hipóteses que eu poderia ver da rua.
Não há na travessa achada número de porta que me deram.   10

Acordei para a mesma vida para que tinha adormecido.
Até os meus exércitos sonhados sofreram derrota.
Até os meus sonhos se sentiram falsos ao serem sonhados.
Até a vida só desejada me farta—até essa vida . . .

Compreendo a intervalos desconexos;   15
Escrevo por lapsos de cansaço;
E um tédio que é até do tédio arroja-me à praia.

Não sei que destino ou futuro compete à minha angústia sem
    leme;
Não sei que ilhas do Sul impossível aguardam-me náufrago;
Ou que palmares de literatura me darão ao menos um verso.   20

Não, não sei isto, nem outra coisa, nem coisa nenhuma . . .
E, no fundo do meu espírito, onde sonho o que sonhei,
Nos campos últimos da alma, onde memoro sem causa
(E o passado é uma névoa natural de lágrimas falsas),
Nas estradas e atalhos das florestas longínquas   25
Onde supus o meu ser,
Fogem desmantelados, últimos restos
Da ilusão final,
Os meus exércitos sonhados, derrotados sem ter sido,
As minhas coortes por existir, esfaceladas em Deus.   30

Outra vez te revejo,
Cidade da minha infância pavorosamente perdida . . .
Cidade triste e alegre, outra vez sonho aqui . . .
Eu? Mas sou eu o mesmo que aqui vivi, e aqui voltei,
E aqui tornei a voltar, e a voltar.   35
E aqui de novo tornei a voltar?   *over*

With the anguish of one ravenous for meat, I yearn
For something, I don't know what—
Definitely for the indefinite . . .   *5*
Restlessly asleep, I live in the restless dream-state
Of one restlessly asleep, half in a dream.

Every abstract door I needed has been closed to me.
The curtains have been drawn over every hypothesis I might
    see from the street.
When I find the right side-street, the number I was given
    isn't there.   *10*

The life I fell asleep to was the same when I awoke.
Even the armies I dreamed of suffered defeat.
Even my dreams felt false in the dreaming.
Even the life I merely desire brings satiety—even *that* life . . .

I understand at unrelated moments;   *15*
I write between spells of weariness;
And the very boredom of being bored casts me up on the beach.

I don't know what fate or future lies in store for my drifting
    anguish;
I don't know what islands of the unattainable South await me
    as a castaway;
Nor what literary palm-groves will at least give me a line of verse.

No, I don't know that, nor anything else, nor anything at all . . .
And in the depths of my spirit, where I dream what I dreamt,
In the remotest realms of the soul, where I needlessly remember
(And the past is a natural fog of false tears),
In the highways and by-ways of the far-off forests   *25*
Where I fancied my being was,
The last remnants of the final illusion
Flee in disorder,—
The armies I dreamed of, routed before they existed,
My could-be cohorts, shattered in God.   *30*

I see you once more,
City of my childhood now frighteningly lost . . .
City mournful and gay, once more in you I dream . . .
I do? But am I the same one who lived here, and came back,
And came back again, and again?   *35*
And did I really come back again?

Ou somos todos os Eu que estive aqui ou estiveram,
Uma série de contas-entes ligadas por um fio-memória,
Uma série de sonhos de mim de alguém de fora de mim?

Outra vez te revejo,   40
Com o coração mais longínquo, a alma menos minha.

Outra vez te revejo—Lisboa e Tejo e tudo—,
Transeunte inútil de ti e de mim,
Estrangeiro aqui como em toda a parte,
Casual na vida como na alma,   45
Fantasma a errar em salas de recordações,
Ao ruído dos ratos e das tábuas que rangem
No castelo maldito de ter que viver . . .

Outra vez te revejo,
Sombra que passa através de sombras, e brilha   50
Um momento a uma luz fúnebre desconhecida,
E entra na noite como um rastro de barço se perde
Na água que deixa de se ouvir . . .

Outra vez te revejo,
Mas, ai, a mim não me revejo!   55
Partiu-se o espelho mágico em que me revia idêntico,
E em cada fragmento fatídico vejo só um bocado de mim—
Um bocado de ti e de mim! . . .

22)   Se te queres matar, porque não te queres matar?
       Ah, aproveita! que eu, que tanto amo a morte e a vida,
       Se ousasse matar-me, também me mataria . . .
       Ah, se ousares, ousa!
       De que te serve o quadro sucessivo das imagens externas   5
       A que chamamos o mundo?
       A cinematografia das horas representadas
       Por actores de convenções e poses determinadas,
       O circo policromo do nosso dinamismo sem fim?
       De que te serve o teu mundo interior que desconheces?   10
       Talvez, matando-te, o conheças finalmente . . .
       Talvez, acabando, comeces . . .
       E, de qualquer forma, se te cansa seres,
       Ah, cansa-te nobremente,   *over*

Or are all of us that self, those selves who were here,
A string of bead-lives threaded by memory,
A string of dreams about me by someone outside myself?

I see you once more,   *40*
With my heart more remote and my soul less my own.

I see you once more—Lisbon and Tagus and all—,
A pointless passer-by to you and to me,
As much a foreigner here as anywhere,
A chance event in life as in the soul,   *45*
A ghost roaming through halls of reminiscence,
To the scurrying of mice and the creaking of boards
In the doom-laden castle of having to live . . .

I see you once more,
A shadow moving through shadows, lit   *50*
For a moment by a gloomy unfamiliar glow,
Then passing into night like the waning wake of a boat
As the water subsides into silence . . .

I see you once more;
If only I could see *myself* once more!   *55*
The magic mirror shattered where I saw myself unchanged,
And in each fateful fragment I see only a piece of me—
A piece of you, a piece of me! . . .

22) If you want to kill yourself, why don't you want to kill yourself?
      Well, now's your chance! For I, who dearly love both death and
         life,
      Would kill myself too, if I only dared.
      Well, do you dare or don't you?
      What use to you is this tale of outward images in sequence   *5*
      Known to us as the world?
      This film-show featuring the hours performed
      By actors with fixed poses and conventions,
      This motley circus of our endless urges?
      What use to you that inner world of self you know so badly?   *10*
      Kill yourself: perhaps you'll get to know it better . . .
      Perhaps by ending you'll begin . . .
      And if you find existence tiring,
      Well, at least get tired with dignity,

E não cantes, como eu, a vida por bebedeira,   *15*
Não saúdes como eu a morte em literatura!

Fazes falta? Ó sombra fútil chamada gente!
Ninguém faz falta; não fazes falta a ninguém . . .
Sem ti correrá tudo sem ti.
Talvez seja pior para outros existires que matares-te . . .   *20*
Talvez peses mais durando, que deixando de durar . . .

A mágoa dos outros? Tens remorso adiantado
De que te chorem?
Descansa: pouco te chorarão . . .
O impulso vital apaga as lágrimas pouco a pouco,   *25*
Quando não são de coisas nossas,
Quando são do que acontece aos outros, sobretudo a morte,
Porque é a coisa depois da qual nada acontece aos outros . . .

Primeiro é a angústia, a surpresa da vinda
Do mistério e da falta da tua vida falada . . .   *30*
Depois o horror do caixão visível e material,
E os homens de preto que exercem a profissão de estar ali.
Depois a família a velar, inconsolável e contando anedotas,
Lamentando a pena de teres morrido,
E tu mera causa ocasional daquela carpidação,   *35*
Tu verdadeiramente morto, muito mais morto que calculas . . .
Muito mais morto aqui que calculas,
Mesmo que estejas muito mais vivo além . . .
Depois a trágica retirada para o jazigo ou a cova,
E depois o princípio da morte da tua memória.   *40*
Há primeiro em todos um alívio
Da tragédia um pouco maçadora de teres morrido . . .
Depois a conversa aligeira-se quotidianamente,
E a vida de todos os dias retoma o seu dia . . .

Depois, lentamente esqueceste.   *45*
Só és lembrado em duas datas, aniversàriamente:
Quando faz anos que nasceste, quando faz anos que morreste.
Mais nada, mais nada, absolutamente mais nada.
Duas vezes no ano pensam em ti.   *over*

And don't, as I do, sing of life because you're drunk;   *15*
Don't, as I do, welcome death on paper!

You're needed? What, by those vain shadows we call people?
Nobody's needed: nobody needs you.
If you're not here, things will go on without you.
It may be worse for others if you live than if you kill yourself: *20*
You may be a heavier cross if you endure than if you stop
    enduring.

Others would mourn? Are you sorry in advance
That they should weep for you?
Don't worry: they won't weep for long . . .
Bit by bit the urge to live will put an end to tears,   *25*
When they're not shed for *our* affairs,
When they're shed for what happens to others—death above all,
For that is the end of what happens to others.

First there's the anguish when the mystery comes
Unlooked-for, and your life isn't news any more;   *30*
Then visible and real the horror of the coffin,
With the men in black professionally present.
Then the family at the wake, telling funny stories in their
    heartbreak,
As they mourn for the pity of your death.
And you?—The mere immediate cause of all those sobs and tears.
You?—*Really* dead, far deader than you think;
Far deader on this side than you think,
Even though you may be more alive in the beyond.
Then it's the tragic retreat to the grave or to the vault,
And then the memory of you begins to die.   *40*
At first they all feel a sense of relief
From that faintly boring tragedy, your death;
Then day by day the talk becomes more cheerful;
Life with its daily round soon takes its turn again.

Then you were slowly forgotten.   *45*
There are only two days in the year when you're remembered
    now:
The day you came into the world, the day you breathed your last.
No more, no more, no more than just that.
Twice a year they think of you.

Duas vezes no ano suspiram por ti os que te amaram,   50
E uma ou outra vez suspiram se por acaso se fala em ti.

Encara-te a frio, e encara a frio o que somos . . .
Se queres matar-te, mata-te . . .
Não tenhas escrúpulos morais, receios de inteligência ! . . .
Que escrúpulos ou receios tem a mecânica da vida ?   55
Que escrúpulos químicos tem o impulso que gera
As seivas, e a circulação do sangue, e o amor ?
Que memória dos outros tem o ritmo alegre da vida ?
Ah, pobre vaidade de carne e osso chamado homem,
Não vês que não tens importância absolutamente nenhuma ?   60

És importante para ti, porque é a ti que te sentes.
És tudo para ti, porque para ti és o universo,
E o próprio universo e os outros
Satélites da tua subjectividade objectiva.
És importante para ti porque só tu és importante para ti.   65
E se és assim, ó mito, não serão os outros assim ?

Tens, como Hamlet, o pavor do desconhecido ?
Mas o que é conhecido ? O que é que tu conheces,
Para que chames desconhecido a qualquer coisa em especial ?
Tens, como Falstaff, o amor gorduroso da vida ?   70
Se assim a amas materialmente, ama-a ainda mais materialmente:
Torna-te parte carnal da terra e das coisas !
Dispersa-te, sistema físico-químico
De células nocturnamente conscientes
Pela nocturna consciência da inconsciência dos corpos,   75
Pelo grande cobertor não-cobrindo-nada das aparências,
Pela relva e a erva da proliferação dos seres,
Pela névoa atómica das coisas,
Pelas paredes turbilhonantes
Do vácuo dinâmico do mundo . . .   80

23)   *Tabacaria*

Não sou nada.
Nunca serei nada.
Não posso querer ser nada.
À parte isso, tenho em mim todos os sonhos do mundo.

over

Twice a year the ones who loved you heave a sigh for you,   *50*
And now and then they heave a sigh if your name comes up by
    chance.

Face yourself squarely: squarely face what we are . . .
If you want to kill yourself, why don't you?
No moral scruples, no intellectual fears!
Are there scruples or fears in the way life goes on?   *55*
Are there chemical scruples in the impulse which begets
Sap, the circulating blood, and love?
Are there memories of others in the joyous rhythm of life?
Oh you poor vanity of flesh and bone called man,
Can't you see you just don't count at all?   *60*

You matter to you, because you're the one you feel.
You're everything to you: you're your own universe.
And the real universe, and other people?
Mere satellites to your objective subjectivity!
You matter to you, because *only you* matter to you.   *65*
And if you're like that, you myth, won't others be the same?

Do you, like Hamlet, stand in dread of the unknown?
But what is known? What do you know,
That you should say 'unknown' of this rather than that?
Do you, like Falstaff, love life with all your fat?   *70*
If you love it so grossly, love it more grossly yet:
Become a fleshly part of the earth and of things!
Scatter your physico-chemical system
Of cells nocturnally conscious
Over the nocturnal consciousness of unconscious bodies,   *75*
Over the great blanket of appearances wrapped round nothing,
Over the grass and the turf where creatures teem and breed,
Over the atomic mist of things,
Over the whirling walls
Of the world's dynamic void.   *80*

23)   *Tobacco-Shop*

I'm nothing.
That's all I'll ever be.
Nothing, with no will-power to be something.
With that reservation, my dreams are boundless.

Janelas do meu quarto,　　　　　　　　　　　　　　5
Do meu quarto de um dos milhões do mundo que ninguém
　　sabe quem é
(E se soubessem quem é, o que saberiam?),
Dais para o mistério de uma rua cruzada constantemente por
　　gente,
Para uma rua inacessível a todos os pensamentos,
Real, impossívelmente real, certa, desconhecidamente certa,　　10
Com o mistério das coisas por baixo das pedras e dos seres,
Com a morte a pôr humidade nas paredes e cabelos brancos nos
　　homens,
Com o Destino a conduzir a carroça de tudo pela estrada de nada.
Estou hoje vencido, como se soubesse a verdade.
Estou hoje lúcido, como se estivesse para morrer,　　　　　15
E não tivesse mais irmandade com as coisas
Senão uma despedida, tornando-se esta casa e este lado da rua
A fileira de carruagens de um comboio, e uma partida apitada
De dentro da minha cabeça,
E uma sacudidela dos nervos e um ranger de ossos na ida.　　20

Estou hoje perplexo, como quem pensou e achou e esqueceu.
Estou hoje dividido entre a lealdade que devo
À Tabacaria do outro lado da rua, como coisa real por fora,
E à sensação de que tudo é sonho, como coisa real por dentro.

Falhei em tudo.　　　　　　　　　　　　　　　25
Como não fiz propósito nenhum, talvez tudo fosse nada.
A aprendizagem que me deram,
Desci dela pela janela das traseiras da casa.
Fui até ao campo com grandes propósitos.
Mas lá encontrei só ervas e árvores,　　　　　　　　　30
E quando havia gente era igual à outra.
Saio da janela, sento-me numa cadeira. Em que hei-de pensar?

Que sei eu do que serei, eu que não sei o que sou?
Ser o que penso? Mas penso ser tanta coisa!
E há tantos que pensam ser a mesma coisa que não pode
　　haver tantos!
　　　　　　　　　　　　　　　　　　　　35
Génio? Neste momento
Cem mil cérebros se concebem em sonho génios como eu,

over

You windows in this room of mine,   5
The room of one of the world's millions whose identity no
    one knows
(And if they knew, would they be any the wiser?),
You look out on the mystery of a street with people passing
    all the time,
A street beyond the reach of all thought,
Real, its reality impossible, certain, its certainty unknown,   10
Where mystery underlies stones and beings,
Where death makes walls damp and men's hair white,
Where Fate drives the cart of All along the road to Nothing.
Today I'm beaten, as though I knew the truth.
Today I'm lucid, as though about to die,   15
As though I had no more brotherhood with things
Than saying good-bye, as this house and this side of the street
Turn into a train with a string of carriages pulling out when
    the whistle blows
Inside my head,
With my nerves jarring and my bones creaking as it goes.   20

Today I'm at a loss, like one who thought and found the
    answer, then forgot.
Today I'm torn between my loyalty
To a thing of outward reality—the tobacco-shop across the street,
And to a thing of inward reality,—the feeling that it's all a dream.

I've failed in everything.   25
Since I never had an aim, perhaps what I failed in was nothing.
As for the training they gave me,
I climbed out of it through the back-room window.
I went into the country with great schemes in mind,
But there I found only trees and grass,   30
And when there were people, they were the same as others.
I move away from the window and sit down on a chair. What
    shall I think about?

How should I know what I'll be, when I don't even know what
    I am?
Be what I think I am? But I think I'm so many things,
And there are so many thinking they're the same thing that
    they can't all be right!   35
A genius? At this very moment
A hundred thousand brains are dreaming that they're geniuses
    like me,

E a história não marcará, quem sabe?, nem um,
Nem haverá senão estrume de tantas conquistas futuras.
Não, não creio em mim.   40
Em todos os manicómios há doidos malucos com tantas certezas!
Eu, que não tenho nenhuma certeza, sou mais certo ou menos
  certo?
Não, nem em mim . . .
Em quantas mansardas e não-mansardas do mundo
Não estão nesta hora génios-para-si mesmos sonhando?   45
Quantas aspirações altas e nobres e lúcidas—
Sim, verdadeiramente altas e nobres e lúcidas—,
E quem sabe se realizáveis,
Nunca verão a luz do sol real nem acharão ouvidos de gente?
O mundo é para quem nasce para o conquistar   50
E não para quem sonha que pode conquistá-lo, ainda que tenha
  razão.
Tenho sonhado mais que o que Napoleão fez.
Tenho apertado ao peito hipotético mais humanidades do que
  Cristo,
Tenho feito filosofias em segredo que nenhum Kant escreveu.
Mas sou, e talvez serei sempre, o da mansarda,   55
Ainda que não more nela;
Serei sempre *o que não nasceu para isso;*
Serei sempre só *o que tinha qualidades;*
Serei sempre o que esperou que lhe abrissem a porta ao pé de
  uma parede sem porta
E cantou a cantiga do Infinito numa capoeira,   60
E ouviu a voz de Deus num poço tapado.
Crer em mim? Não, nem em nada.
Derrame-me a Natureza sobre a cabeça ardente
O seu sol, a sua chuva, o vento que me acha o cabelo,
E o resto que venha se vier, ou tiver que vir, ou não venha. 65
Escravos cardíacos das estrelas,
Conquistámos todo o mundo antes de nos levantar da cama;
Mas acordámos e ele é opaco,
Levantámo-nos e ele é alheio,
Saímos de casa e ele é a terra inteira,   70
Mais o sistema solar e a Via Láctea e o Indefinido.

(Come chocolates, pequena;
Come chocolates!
                                                    over

Yet history is unlikely to record a single name,
And all those would-be conquests will be so much chaff, no more.
No, I don't believe in myself.   *40*
Every asylum has its crazy fools brim-full of certainty!
I'm certain of nothing: does that make me more certain, or less?
No, not even in myself . . .
Is there a single garret or non-garret in this world
That hasn't a self-styled genius dreaming inside it right now?   *45*
How many lofty, noble, lucid aspirations—
Yes, truly lofty, noble and lucid—,
(And for all we know they might even be fulfilled)
Will never see the true light of day, nor find a hearing?
The world is for the one born to conquer it,   *50*
Not for the one who dreams he can, even if he's right.
In dreams I've achieved more than Napoleon.
I've clasped to my hypothetical breast more human races
    than Christ,
I've secretly devised philosophies no Kant ever wrote.
Yet I'll probably always be what I am now, the fellow in the
    garret,   *55*
Though I don't live there;
I'll always be the one who *wasn't born for that*;
I'll always just be the one who *had it in him*;
I'll always be the one who waited for the door to open in the
    doorless wall,
Who sang the song of Infinity in a hen-coop,   *60*
And heard the voice of God in a covered well.
Believe in myself? No, nor in anything else.
Let Nature pour over my fevered head
Her sunshine, her rain, the wind I can feel in my hair,
And let the rest come if it will, or come if it must, or not come
    at all.   *65*
Cardiac slaves of the stars,
We've conquered the whole world before we get out of bed,
But once we're awake it's inscrutable,
Once we're up it's foreign,
Once we're out of doors it's the whole earth,   *70*
Plus the Solar System, the Milky Way and Infinite Space.

(Eat those chocolates, little girl;
Eat those chocolates!

Olha que não há mais metafísica no mundo senão chocolates.
Olha que as religiões todas não ensinam mais que a confeitaria. *75*
Come, pequena suja, come!
Pudesse eu comer chocolates com a mesma verdade com que
  comes!
Mas eu penso e, ao tirar o papel de prata, que é de folha de
  estanho,
Deito tudo para o chão, como tenho deitado a vida.)

Mas ao menos fica da amargura do que nunca serei   *80*
A caligrafia rápida destes versos,
Pórtico partido para o Impossível.
Mas ao menos consagro a mim mesmo um desprezo sem lágrimas,
Nobre ao menos no gesto largo com que atiro
A roupa suja que sou, sem rol, pra o decurso das coisas,   *85*
E fico em casa sem camisa.

(Tu, que consolas, que não existes e por isso consolas,
  Ou deusa grega, concebida como estátua que fosse viva,
  Ou patrícia romana, impossìvelmente nobre e nefasta,
  Ou princesa de trovadores, gentilíssima e colorida,   *90*
  Ou marquesa do século dezoito, decotada e longínqua,
  Ou cocote célebre do tempo dos nossos pais,
  Ou não sei quê moderno—não concebo bem o quê—,
  Tudo isso, seja o que for, que sejas, se pode inspirar que inspire!
  Meu coração é um balde despejado.   *95*
  Como os que invocam espíritos invocam espíritos invoco
  A mim mesmo e não encontro nada.
  Chego à janela e vejo a rua com uma nitidez absoluta.
  Vejo as lojas, vejo os passeios, vejo os carros que passam,
  Vejo os entes vivos vestidos que se cruzam,   *100*
  Vejo os cães que também existem,
  E tudo isto me pesa como uma condenação ao degredo,
  E tudo isto é estrangeiro, como tudo.)

Vivi, estudei, amei, e até cri,
E hoje não há mendigo que eu não inveje só por não ser eu.   *105*
Olho a cada um os andrajos e as chagas e a mentira,
E penso: talvez nunca vivesses nem estudasses nem amasses
  nem cresses

over

Take it from me, chocolates are the only metaphysics in the world.
Take it from me, all religions put together teach us no more than
    a sweet-shop does.   *75*
Eat them, you little beast, eat them!
I wish I could eat chocolates as truly as you do!
But I think, and when I've unwrapped the silver paper, tinfoil
    in point of fact,
I throw the whole lot on the ground, just as I've thrown away
    my life.)

Yet, from the bitterness of what I'll never be, at least remains   *80*
The hasty penning of this poem,
A ruined gateway to the Impossible;
At least the contempt I bestow on myself is dry-eyed,
At least there's dignity in the grand gesture with which I fling
The dirty linen that's myself—no list attached—into the march
    of time,   *85*
And stay at home, shirtless.

(Oh great consoler, non-existent and therefore consoling,
    Whether you be Greek goddess conceived as a statue, but alive,
    Or Roman dame, impossibly dignified and fatal,
    Or princess sung by minstrels, all *courtoisie* and colour,   *90*
    Or eighteenth-century marquise, remote in her low dress,
    Or famous courtesan of the last generation,
    Or something modern—I'm not quite sure just what—
    Anyway, if whatever you are can inspire, let it inspire me now!
    My heart is a bucket that's been emptied.   *95*
    As those who invoke spirits invoke spirits I invoke
    Myself and find nothing there.
    Going to the window, I can see the street with stark lucidity.
    I can see shops and pavements and passing cars,
    I can see clothed human beings walking past each other,   *100*
    I can see dogs, for they exist too,
    And all this grieves me like a sentence of banishment,
    And all this is as foreign as everything is.)

I've lived and studied, loved and even believed,
And now there's not a beggar I don't envy just because he isn't me.
I see the rags, the sores, the lies of each of them,
And say to myself: perhaps you never lived or studied, loved
    or believed

(Porque é possível fazer a realidade de tudo isso sem fazer
   nada disso);
Talvez tenhas existido apenas, como um lagarto a quem
   cortam o rabo
E que é rabo para aquém do lagarto remexidamente.   *110*

Fiz de mim o que não soube,
E o que podia fazer de mim não o fiz.
O dominó que vesti era errado.
Conheceram-me logo por quem não era e não desmenti, e
   perdi-me.
Quando quis tirar a máscara,   *115*
Estava pegada à cara.
Quando a tirei e me vi ao espelho,
Já tinha envelhecido.
Estava bêbado, já não sabia vestir o dominó que não tinha tirado.
Deitei fora a máscara e dormi no vestiário   *120*
Como um cão tolerado pela gerência
Por ser inofensivo
E vou escrever esta historia para provar que sou sublime.

Essência musical dos meus versos inúteis,
Quem me dera encontrar-te como coisa que eu fizesse,   *125*
E não ficasse sempre defronte da Tabacaria de defronte,
Calcando aos pés a consciência de estar existindo,
Como um tapete em que um bêbado tropeça
Ou um capacho que os ciganos roubaram e não valia nada.

Mas o Dono da Tabacaria chegou à porta e ficou à porta.   *130*
Olho-o com o desconforto da cabeça mal voltada
E com o desconforto da alma mal-entendendo.
Ele morrerá e eu morrerei.
Ele deixará a tabuleta, e eu deixarei versos.
A certa altura morrerá a tabuleta também, e os versos também.
Depois de certa altura morrerá a rua onde esteve a tabuleta,

E a língua em que foram escritos os versos.
Morrerá depois o planeta girante em que tudo isto se deu.
Em outros satélites de outros sistemas qualquer coisa como gente
Continuará fazendo coisas como versos e vivendo por baixo
   de coisas como tabuletas,
     140
Sempre uma coisa defronte da outra,
Sempre uma coisa tão inútil como a outra,   *over*

(For we can do all this in reality without doing it at all);
Perhaps you just existed, as when a lizard has its tail cut off,
And the tail's all wriggly, but short of a lizard.   *110*

I became what I couldn't,
And what I might have become, I didn't.
I put on someone else's fancy dress.
They knew me at once for the one I wasn't: I didn't contradict
    them, and was lost.
When I tried to take off the mask,   *115*
It was stuck to my face.
When I took it off and saw myself in the glass,
I had grown old.
I was drunk and couldn't put on the fancy dress I hadn't taken off.
I threw away the mask and slept in the cloak-room   *120*
Like a dog allowed in by the management
Because it's harmless,
And I'm going to write this story to prove I'm sublime.

Oh musical essence of my pointless verse,
If only I could find you as something I created,   *125*
Instead of forever facing the tobacco-shop over opposite,
And treading on the awareness of my own existence
As though it were a rug on which a drunkard stumbles
Or a door-mat stolen by gypsies and not worth stealing.

But the Tobacconist comes to his door and stands there.   *130*
I look at him with my head uncomfortably half-turned
And my spirit uncomfortably half-comprehending.
He will die and I shall die.
He will leave his signboard: I shall leave my poetry.
In time the signboard will die too, and so will my poetry.   *135*
A time will come when the street the signboard was in will
    die too,

So will the language my poetry was written in.
Then the whirling planet will die, where all this took place.
In other satellites in other systems something resembling people
Will go on doing things like writing poetry and living under
    things like signboards,   *140*
Forever one thing facing another,
Forever one thing as pointless as the next,

Sempre o impossível tão estúpido como o real,
Sempre o mistério do fundo tão certo como o sono de mistério
     da superfície,
Sempre isto ou sempre outra coisa ou nem uma coisa nem outra.

Mas um homem entrou na Tabacaria (para comprar tabaco?),
E a realidade plausível cai de repente em cima de mim.
Semiergo-me enérgico, convencido, humano,
E vou tencionar escrever estes versos em que digo o contrário.
Acendo um cigarro ao pensar em escrevê-los   *150*
E saboreio no cigarro a libertação de todos os pensamentos.
Sigo o fumo como uma rota própria,
E gozo, num momento sensitivo e competente,
A libertação de todas as especulações
E a consciência de que a metafísica é uma consequência de
     estar mal disposto.   *155*

Depois deito-me para trás na cadeira
E continuo fumando.
Enquanto o Destino mo conceder, continuarei fumando.

(Se eu casasse com a filha da minha lavadeira
     Talvez fosse feliz.)   *160*
Visto isto, levanto-me da cadeira. Vou à janela.

O homem saiu da Tabacaria (metendo troco na algibeira das
     calças?).
Ah, conheço-o: é o Esteves sem metafísica.
(O Dono da Tabacaria chegou à porta.)
Como por um instinto divino o Esteves voltou-se e viu-me.   *165*
Acenou-me adeus, gritei-lhe *Adeus ó Esteves!*, e o universo
Reconstruiu-se-me sem ideal nem esperança, e o Dono da
     Tabacaria sorriu.

24) *Demogorgon*

Na rua cheia de sol vago há casas paradas e gente que anda.
Uma tristeza cheia de pavor esfria-me.
Pressinto um acontecimento do lado de lá das frontarias e dos
     movimentos.

                                                        over

Forever impossibility as stupid as reality,
Forever mystery deep down as certain as mystery sleeping
    on the surface,
Forever this, forever that, or neither one thing nor the other.   *145*

But a man goes into the tobacco-shop (to buy tobacco?),
And plausible reality suddenly dawns on me.
Vigorous, sure of myself, a man again, I half rise to my feet,
And I shall try to write this poem in which I say the opposite.
I light a cigarette as I think about writing it,   *150*
And in that cigarette I relish my total release from having to
    think.
I follow the smoke as though it were a private tour,
And enjoy in a suitable and sensitive moment
My release from any kind of speculation
As I realize that metaphysics comes of feeling ill.   *155*

Then I throw myself back in my chair
And go on smoking.
As long as Fate lets me, I shall go on smoking.

(If I were to marry my washerwoman's daughter
    I might be happy).   *160*
With this, I get up from my chair and go to the window.

Now the man comes out of the tobacco-shop (putting change
    in his trouser-pocket?).
Ah yes, I know him: it's the unmetaphysical Esteves.
(The Tobacconist appears at his door.)
As if prompted by some divine instinct Esteves turns round
    and sees me.   *165*
He waves good-bye, I call out 'Good-bye, Esteves'. The universe
Falls into place for me again with no ideals or hopes, and
    the Tobacconist smiles.

24)   *Demogorgon*

Dim sunlight floods the street where houses stand and people
    walk.
Chilled by a sadness charged with dread,
I sense something about to happen beyond the housefronts
    and the walking.

Não, não, isso não!
Tudo menos saber o que é o Mistério!   5
Superfície do Universo, ó Pálpebras Descidas,
Não vos ergais nunca!
O olhar da Verdade Final não deve poder suportar-se!

Deixai-me viver sem saber nada, e morrer sem ir saber nada!
A razão de haver ser, a razão de haver seres, de haver tudo,   10
Deve trazer uma loucura maior que os espaços
Entre as almas e entre as estrelas.

Não, não, a verdade não! Deixai-me estas casas e esta gente;
Assim mesmo, sem mais nada, estas casas e esta gente . . .
Que abafo horrível e frio me toca em olhos fechados?   15
Não os quero abrir de viver! Ó Verdade, esquece-te de mim!

25)   Na noite terrível, substância natural de todas as noites,
Na noite de insónia, substância natural de todas as minhas noites,
Relembro, velando em modorra incómoda,
Relembro o que fiz e o que podia ter feito na vida.
Relembro, e uma angústia   5
Espalha-se por mim todo como um frio do corpo ou um medo.
O irreparável do meu passado—esse é que é o cadáver!
Todos os outros cadáveres pode ser que sejam ilusão.
Todos os mortos pode ser que sejam vivos noutra parte.
Todos os meus próprios momentos passados pode ser que
    existam algures,   10
Na ilusão do espaço e do tempo,
Na falsidade do decorrer.
Mas o que eu não fui, o que eu não fiz, o que nem sequer sonhei;
O que só agora vejo que deveria ter feito,
O que só agora claramente vejo que deveria ter sido—   15
Isso é que é morto para além de todos os deuses,
Isso—e foi afinal o melhor de mim—é que nem os deuses
    fazem viver . . .

Se em certa altura
Tivesse voltado para a esquerda em vez de para a direita;
Se em certo momento
Tivesse dito sim em vez de não, ou não em vez de sim;   20
Se em certa conversa
Tivesse tido as frases que só agora, no meio-sono, elaboro—

over

No, no, not that!
Anything but knowledge of the Mystery!   5
Oh Lowered Eyelids, Surface of the Universe,
Remain forever closed!
The gaze of Ultimate Truth can surely not be borne!

Oh let me live in ignorance, and die knowing nothing!
The reason for existence, the reason for beings, for everything,   *10*
Must mean a madness greater than the distance
From soul to soul, from star to star.

No, no, not the truth! Leave me these houses and these people;
No more than just this, these houses and these people . . .
What chill and awful breath is this, that touches my closed eyes?
I will not open them from life! Oh Truth, *forget me*!

25)   In the terror of night—the stuff all nights are made of,
In the sleeplessness of night—the stuff my nights are made of,
I remember, awake in irksome lethargy,
I remember what I did and could have done with life,
I remember, and anguish   5
Pervades my being like a creeping fear or chill.
My irremediable past—that's the corpse on my hands!
All other corpses may be just illusions.
All the dead may live on somewhere else.
All my past moments may exist elsewhere,   *10*
In the illusion of time and space,
In the mirage of unfolding events.
But what I never was, what I never did, what I never even
      dreamed;
What I see only now that I ought to have done,
See clearly only now that I ought to have been—   *15*
It's *that* that's dead beyond the gods' recalling,
And though it was the best of me, not even they can give it
      life . . .

If at some point in time
I had turned left instead of right;
If at some moment   20
I had said yes instead of no, or no instead of yes;
If, in conversation,
I had used the words which only now I drowsily devise—

Se tudo isso tivesse sido assim,
Seria outro hoje, e talvez o universo inteiro   *25*
Seria insensìvelmente levado a ser outro também.

Mas não virei para o lado irreparàvelmente perdido,
Não virei nem pensei em virar, e só agora o percebo;
Mas não disse não ou não disse sim, e só agora vejo o que não disse;
Mas as frases que faltou dizer nesse momento surgem-me todas,
Claras, inevitáveis, naturais,
A conversa fechada concludentemente,
A matéria toda resolvida . . .
Mas só agora o que nunca foi, nem será para trás, me dói.
O que falhei deveras não tem esperança nenhuma   *35*
Em sistema metafísico nenhum.
Pode ser que para outro mundo eu possa levar o que sonhei,
Mas poderei eu levar para outro mundo o que me esqueci de
    sonhar?
Esses sim, os sonhos por haver, é que são o cadáver.
Enterro-o no meu coração para sempre, para todo o tempo,
    para todos os universos,
Nesta noite em que não durmo, e o sossego me cerca   *40*
Como uma verdade de que não partilho,
E lá fora o luar, como a esperança que não tenho, é invisível
    p'ra mim.

26) *Aniversário*

No tempo em que festejavam o dia dos meus anos,
Eu era feliz e ninguém estava morto.
Na casa antiga, até eu fazer anos era uma tradição de há
    séculos,
E a alegria de todos, e a minha, estava certa como uma religião
    qualquer.

No tempo em que festejavam o dia dos meus anos,   *5*
Eu tinha a grande saúde de não perceber coisa nenhuma,
De ser inteligente para entre a família,
E de não ter as esperanças que os outros tinham por mim.
Quando vim a ter esperanças, já não sabia ter esperanças.
Quando vim a olhar para a vida, perdera o sentido da vida.   *10*

Sim, o que fui de suposto a mim mesmo,
O que fui de corãção, e parentesco,   *over*

If all that had been so,
I'd be different now, and perhaps the universe itself   *25*
Would be subtly induced to be different too.

But I didn't take that turning, now irreparably lost,
Didn't turn or think of turning, and I know it only now;
Didn't say no or didn't say yes, and I see only now what I
   failed to say;
But all the words then left unsaid rise up before me now,   *30*
Clear, inescapable and obvious,
Conversations clinched and ended,
Subjects settled once for all . . .
But all that never was, nor will have been, hurts now for the
   first time.
There's no hope at all for what I didn't do,   *35*
In any metaphysics you can think of.
I could take what I dreamed to another world, perhaps,
But could I take what I *forgot* to dream?
It's those—the dreams undreamt—it's those that are the corpse.
I bury it forever in my heart, for all time, for all worlds,   *40*
On this night when I can't sleep, and peace surrounds me
Like a truth I have no share in,
And I can no more see the moonlight out there than the hope
   I haven't got.

26) *Birthday*

In the days when my birthday was still an event,
I was happy and no one had died.
In the old house, even my birthdays were an age-old tradition,
And for me and for all, joy was as sure as any religion.

In the days when my birthday was still an event,   *5*
I was far too healthy to understand things,
Was intelligent—within the family circle,
And didn't share the hopes which others had for me.
When I first hoped, I had forgotten how to hope.
When I first looked at life, life had lost its meaning for me.   *10*

Yes, what my idea of myself meant to me,
What my inmost feelings, what my family meant to me,

O que fui de serões de meia-província,
O que fui de amarem-me e eu ser menino,
O que fui—ai, meu Deus!, o que só hoje sei que fui . . .   15
A que distância! . . .
(Nem o acho . . .)
O tempo em que festejavam o dia dos meus anos!

O que eu sou hoje é como a humidade no corredor do fim da casa,
Pondo grelado nas paredes . . .   20
O que eu sou hoje (e a casa dos que me amaram treme através
   das minhas lágrimas),
O que eu sou hoje é terem vendido a casa,
É terem morrido todos,
É estar eu sobrevivente a mim-mesmo como um fósforo frio . . .

No tempo em que festejavam o dia dos meus anos . . .   25
Que meu amor, como uma pessoa, esse tempo!
Dessejo físico da alma de se encontrar ali outra vez,
Por uma viagem metafísica e carnal,
Com uma dualidade de eu para mim . . .
Comer o passado como pão de fome, sem tempo de manteiga
   nos dentes!   30

Vejo tudo outra vez com uma nitidez que me cega para o que
   há aqui . . .
A mesa posta com mais lugares, com melhores desenhos na
   loiça, com mais copos,
O aparador com muitas coisas—doces, frutas, o resto na sombra
   debaixo do alçado—,
As tias velhas, os primos diferentes, e tudo era por minha causa,
No tempo em que festejavam o dia dos meus anos . . .   35

Pára, meu coração!
Não penses! Deixa o pensar na cabeça!
Ó meu Deus, meu Deus, meu Deus!
Hoje já não faço anos.
Duro.   40
Somam-se-me dias.
Serei velho quando o for.
Mais nada.
Raiva de não ter trazido o passado roubado na algibeira! . . .

O tempo em que festejavam o dia dos meus anos! . . .   45

What those country-style evenings at home meant to me,
What their love for myself as a child meant to me,
What they meant to me, dear God!, I see only now . . .   *15*
So far off! . . .
(Beyond my reach . . .)
The days when my birthday was still an event!

What I am now is like the damp in the passage at the back
   of the house,
Making things sprout on the walls . . .   *20*
I'm what I am now (the house of those who loved me
   trembles through my tears),
I'm what I am now because they sold the house,
And they're all dead,
With me surviving myself like a burnt-out match . . .

In the days when my birthday was still an event . . .   *25*
Days dearly beloved, as though they were human!
A physical longing in my soul to be back there again,
To go back there again, in the spirit and in the flesh,
With myself doubling me . . .
To devour the past as a hungry man eats bread—no time for
   butter on my teeth!   *30*

I see it all again, so clearly that I'm blind to what is here . . .
Extra places laid at table, china with nicer patterns, more glasses,
Lots of things on the sideboard—sweets, fruit, and the rest
   in the shadow beneath the shelf—,
Elderly aunts, and various cousins, and all because of me,
In the days when my birthday was still an event . . .   *35*

Stop it, heart of mine!
Don't think! Leave thinking to the head!
Oh God, God, God!
Now I don't have birthdays any more.
I just go on.   *40*
Days add up for me.
I'll be old when the time comes.
That's all.
Oh why didn't I steal the past and bring it with me in my
   pocket? . . .

The days when my birthday was still an event! . . .   *45*

27) Sim, sou eu, eu mesmo, tal qual resultei de tudo,
      Espécie de acessório ou sobresselente próprio,
      Arredores irregulares da minha emoção sincera,
      Sou eu aqui em mim, sou eu.

      Quanto fui, quanto não fui, tudo isso sou.   5
      Quanto quis, quanto não quis, tudo isso me forma.
      Quanto amei ou deixei de amar é a mesma saudade em mim.

      E, ao mesmo tempo, a impressão, um pouco inconsequente,
      Como de um sonho formado sobre realidades mistas,
      De me ter deixado, a mim, num banco de carro eléctrico,   10
      Para ser encontrado pelo acaso de quem se lhe ir sentar em cima.

      E, ao mesmo tempo, a impressão, um pouco longínqua,
      Como de um sonho que se quer lembrar na penumbra a que se
         acorda,
      De haver melhor em mim do que eu.
      Sim, ao mesmo tempo, a impressão, um pouco dolorosa,   15
      Como de um acordar sem sonhos para um dia de muitos credores,
      De haver falhado tudo como tropeçar no capacho,
      De haver embrulhado tudo como a mala sem as escovas,
      De haver substituído qualquer coisa a mim algures na vida.

      Baste! É a impressão um tanto ou quanto metafísica,   20
      Como o sol pela última vez sobre a janela da casa a abandonar,
      De que mais vale ser criança que querer compreender o mundo—
      A impressão de pão com manteiga e brinquedos
      De um grande sossego sem Jardins de Prosérpina,
      De uma boa vontade para com a vida encostada de testa à janela,
      Num ver chover com som lá fora
      E não as lágrimas mortas de custar a engolir.

      Baste, sim baste! Sou eu mesmo, o trocado,
      O emissário sem carta nem credenciais,
      O palhaço sem riso, o bobo com o grande fato de outro,   30
      A quem tinem as campainhas da cabeça

      Como chocalhos pequenos de uma servidão em cima.

      Sou eu mesmo, a charada sincopada
      Que ninguém da roda decifra nos serões de província.

      Sou eu mesmo, que remédio! . . .   35

27) Yes, here I am, the outcome of it all,
       A kind of accessory, a special spare part,
       An anomalous setting for my heart-felt emotions,
       Here I am inside myself, me!

       All I was, all I was not, made me what I am.   *5*
       All I wanted, all I didn't want, gives me my present shape.
       All I loved, all I stopped loving, fills me with the same longing.

       And at the same time, the rather perverse feeling—
       Like a dream based on a jumble of facts—
       That I've left myself behind on a seat in a tram,   *10*
       To be found by whoever happens to go and sit there.

       And at the same time, the rather remote feeling—
       Like a dream vainly recalled in the half-light of awakening—
       That inside me there's something better than myself.
       Yes, at the same time, the rather painful feeling—   *15*
       Like waking from dreamless sleep to a day full of creditors—
       That I've bungled it all like tripping over the mat,
       That I've packed it all like a suitcase—forgetting the brushes,
       That I've substituted something for myself somewhere in life.

       No more! It's the more or less transcendental feeling—   *20*
       Like the sun for the last time on the windows of a house soon
           to be left,—
       That it's better to be a child than try to understand the world,—
       A feeling of bread and butter, and of toys,
       Of profound peace with no gardens of Proserpina,
       Of good-will towards life as it presses its face against the window,
       While rain can be seen audibly falling outside,
       Rain, not those vanished tears, so painful to swallow.

       No more, I say, no more! Here I am, the substitute,
       The envoy with no letter or credentials,
       The solemn clown, the buffoon in someone else's outsize suit,   *30*
       With bells tinkling on his head

       Like tiny cattle-bells of bondage there on top.

       Here I am, the conundrum
       That keeps them all guessing at provincial parties.

       Here I am—can't help it! . . .   *35*

28)   *Realidade*

Sim, passava aqui frequentemente há vinte anos . . .
Nada está mudado—ou, pelo menos, não dou por isso—
Nesta localidade da cidade . . .

Há vinte anos! . . .
O que eu era então! Ora, era outro . . .   5
Há vinte anos, e as casas não sabem de nada . . .

Vinte anos inúteis (e sei lá se o foram!
Sei eu o que é útil ou inútil?) . . .
Vinte anos perdidos (mas o que seria ganhá-los?)

Tento reconstruir na minha imaginação   10
Quem eu era e como era quando por aqui passava
Há vinte anos . . .
Não me lembro, não me posso lembrar.

O outro que aqui passava então,
Se existisse hoje, talvez se lembrasse . . .   15
Há tanta personagem de romance que conheço melhor por dentro
De que esse eu-mesmo que há vinte anos passava aqui!

Sim, o mistério do tempo.
Sim, o não se saber nada,
Sim, o termos todos nascido a bordo.   20
Sim, sim, tudo isso, ou outra forma de o dizer . . .

Daquela janela do segundo-andar, ainda idêntica a si mesma,
Debruçava-se então uma rapariga mais velha que eu, mais
    lembradamente de azul.
Hoje, se calhar, está o quê?
Podemos imaginar tudo do que nada sabemos.   25
Estou parado física e moralmente: não quero imaginar nada . . .

Houve um dia em que subi esta rua pensando alegremente no futuro,
Pois Deus dá licença que o que não existe seja fortemente
    iluminado.
Hoje, descendo esta rua, nem no passado penso alegremente.

Quando muito, nem penso . . .   30
Tenho a impressão que as duas figuras se cruzaram na rua,
    nem então nem agora,
Mas aqui mesmo, sem tempo a perturbar o cruzamento.

over

28)   *Reality*

Yes, twenty years ago I often came this way.
Nothing has changed—at least, so far as I can see—
In this part of the town.

Twenty years ago!
To think what I was then! Well, I was different   *5*
Twenty years ago, and the houses are none the wiser.

Twenty useless years (how do I know they were useless?
As if I know what's useful or what isn't!)
Twenty lost years (but if they should be gained, what then?).

I try to picture in my mind again   *10*
Who I was, what I was like when I came this way
Twenty years ago . . .
I don't remember, can't remember.

If he, that different one who came this way
Existed now, perhaps he would remember.   *15*
There are characters in novels I know better from inside
Than I know that self who came this way twenty years ago!

Yes, time's a mysterious thing.
Yes, and we know we're nothing.
Yes, and we're all in the same boat from birth.   *20*
Oh yes, all that, or words to that effect.

From that second-storey window, still exactly as it was,
A girl would lean out, older than me and—less obliviously—
      dressed in blue.
I wonder if there's any difference now?
Where we know nothing, we can imagine what we please.   *25*
Physically and morally, I've come to a halt: I'll stop imagining.

One day I walked up this street, thinking gaily of what was
      yet to be,
For God allows the non-existent to be brightly lit.
Now I walk down this street, not even thinking gaily of what *was*.

At best, not even thinking . . .   *30*
I've a feeling those two figures passed each other in the
      street, neither then nor now,
But on this spot, their passing undisturbed by time.

Olhámos indiferentemente um para o outro.
E eu o antigo lá subi a rua imaginando um futuro girassol.
E eu o moderno lá desci a rua não imaginando nada.   *35*

Talvez isto realmente se desse . . .
Verdadeiramente se desse . . .
Sim, carnalmente se desse . . .

Sim, talvez . . .

29) O que há em mim é sobretudo cansaço—
Não disto nem daquilo,
Nem sequer de tudo ou de nada:
Cansaço assim mesmo, ele mesmo,
Cansaço.   *5*

A subtileza das sensações inúteis,
As paixões violentas por coisa nenhuma,
Os amores intensos por o suposto em alguém,
Essas coisas todas—
Essas e o que falta nelas eternamente—;   *10*
Tudo isso faz um cansaço,
Este cansaço,
Cansaço.

Há sem dúvida quem ame o infinito,
Há sem dúvida quem deseje o impossível,   *15*
Há sem dúvida quem não queira nada—
Três tipos de idealistas, e eu nenhum deles:
Porque eu amo infinitamente o finito,
Porque eu desejo impossívelmente o possível,
Porque quero tudo, ou um pouco mais, se puder ser,   *20*
Ou até se não puder ser . . .

E o resultado?
Para eles a vida vivida ou sonhada,
Para eles o sonho sonhado ou vivido,
Para eles a média entre tudo e nada, isto é, isto . . .   *25*
Para mim só um grande, um profundo,
E, ah com que felicidade infecundo, cansaço,
Um supremíssimo cansaço,
Íssimo, íssimo, íssimo,
Cansaço . . .   *30*

We glanced at each other with indifference.
And I, the one from then, went up the street, imagining a
   sunflower yet to be.
And I, the one from now, went down the street, my imagination
   blank.   *35*

Perhaps this really happened,
Truly happened,
Happened in the flesh,

Perhaps so . . .

29) What I feel is tiredness above all—
Not that I'm tired of this or that,
Nor even of everything or nothing:
Tiredness, that's all, just
Tiredness.   *5*

The subtlety of feelings not worth feeling,
Passions fiercely felt for nothing at all,
Ardent love for what we think we see in someone,
All those things—
Those things and what they forever lack,   *10*
All that spells tiredness,
This tiredness,
Tiredness.

There's sure to be someone loving the infinite,
There's sure to be someone longing for the impossible,   *15*
There's sure to be someone wanting nothing—
Three kinds of idealist, and none of them me:
For I love what's finite, infinitely,
For I love what's possible, impossibly,
For I want everything, or a bit more, if it can be done,   *20*
Or even if it can't . . .

What comes of it ?
For them, lives lived or dreamed,
For them, dreams dreamed or lived,
For them, the average of all and nothing, that's what . . .   *25*
For me, just a great, profound,
Blissfully barren tiredness,
Tiredness to end all tiredness,
End all, end all, end all
Tiredness.   *30*

30) Símbolos ? Estou farto de símbolos . . .
Mas dizem-me que tudo é símbolo.
Todos me dizem nada.
Quais símbolos ? Sonhos.
Que o sol seja um símbolo, está bem . . .   5
Que a lua seja um símbolo, está bem . . .
Que a terra seja um símbolo, está bem . . .
Mas quem repara no sol senão quando a chuva cessa,
E ele rompe as nuvens e aponta para trás das costas
Para o azul do céu ?   10
Mas quem repara na lua senão para achar
Bela a luz que ela espalha, e não bem ela ?
Mas quem repara na terra, que é o que pisa ?
Chama terra aos campos, às árvores, aos montes,
Por uma diminuição instintiva,   15
Porque o mar também é terra . . .
Bem, vá, que tudo isso seja símbolo . . .
Mas que símbolo é, não o sol, não a lua, não a terra,
Mas neste poente precoce e azulando-se
O sol entre farrapos finos de nuvens,   20
Enquanto a lua é já vista, mística, no outro lado,
E o que fica da luz do dia
Doura a cabeça da costureira que pára vagamente à esquina
Onde se demorava outrora com o namorado que a deixou ?
Símbolos ? Não quero símbolos . . .   25
Queria—pobre figura de miséria e desamparo!—
Que o namorado voltasse para a costureira.

31) Às vezes tenho ideias felizes,
Ideias sùbitamente felizes, em ideias
E nas palavras em que naturalmente se despegam . . .

Depois de escrever, leio . . .
Porque escrevi isto ?   5
Onde fui buscar isto ?
De onde me veio isto ? Isto é melhor do que eu . . .
Seremos nós neste mundo apenas canetas com tinta
Com que alguém escreve a valer o que nós aqui traçamos ? . . .

30) Symbols? I'm sick of symbols . . .
Yet they tell me everything's a symbol.
They're all telling me nothing.
What symbols? Dreams.
So the sun's a symbol—all right . . .   *5*
So the moon's a symbol—all right . . .
So the earth's a symbol—all right . . .
But who takes any notice of the sun, save when the rain stops,
And it breaks through the clouds, aiming its beams
At the blue sky behind its back?   *10*
But who takes any notice of the moon, save to admire
The light it sheds, and not itself?
But who takes any notice of the earth, when we're standing on it?
When we say 'the earth', we mean fields and trees and hills,
Instinctively belittling it,   *15*
Because the sea's the earth as well.
All right, it's all symbolic then . . .
But what symbol is it—neither sun nor moon nor earth—
When the sun sets too early in a haze of blue
Amid thin and tattered clouds,   *20*
While already on the other side the moon is seen all mystical,
And the last of daylight
Bathes the dressmaker's head in gold as she pauses at the corner
Where she used to linger with the young man who left her?
Symbols? I don't want symbols . . .   *25*
I want to see the dressmaker—poor forlorn unhappy creature—
Get her young man back.

31) I sometimes have lucky ideas,
Ideas suddenly lucky in ideas
And in the words they naturally fall into . . .

I write, and then I read . . .
Why did I write this?   *5*
Where did I get this from?
Where did this come from? It's too good to be mine . . .
What if we in this world should be mere pens and ink
With which someone writes—and means—what we set down
   here?

32)   Os antigos invocavam as Musas.
         Nós invocamo-nos a nós mesmos.
         Não sei se as Musas apareciam—
         Seria sem dúvida conforme o invocado e a invocação.—
         Mas sei que nós não aparecemos.   5
         Quantas vezes me tenho debruçado
         Sobre o poço que me suponho
         E balido 'Ah!' para ouvir um eco,
         E não tenho ouvido mais que o visto—
         O vago alvor escuro com que a água resplandece   10
         Lá na inutilidade do fundo . . .
         Nenhum eco para mim . . .
         Só vagamente uma cara,
         Que deve ser a minha, por não poder ser de outro.
         É uma coisa quase invisível,   15
         Excepto como luminosamente vejo
         Lá no fundo . . .
         No silêncio e na luz falsa do fundo . . .

         Que Musa! . . .

32)   The ancients used to invoke the Muses:
       We invoke ourselves.
       I don't know if the Muses ever came—
       It would of course depend who was invoked and how—
       But *we* don't come, I'm sure of that.   5
       How many times have I peered
       Into the well I fancy that I am
       And plaintively cried 'Aah!', hoping for an echo
       Yet heard no more than what I saw—
       The dim dark brightness of a gleam of water,   10
       Down in the pointless depths . . .
       No echo for me . . .
       Just an ill-defined face
       Which must be mine (if not, whose could it be?).
       It's something I can hardly see at all,   15
       Except as clearly as I see
       Down there . . .
       In the bottom's silence and deceptive light . . .

       Some Muse!

END OF *Campos*

From O GUARDADOR DE REBANHOS

33) XIV

Não me importo com as rimas. Raras vezes
Há duas árvores iguais, uma ao lado da outra.
Penso e escrevo como as flores têm cor
Mas com menos perfeição no meu modo de exprimir-me
Porque me falta a simplicidade divina   *5*
De ser todo só o meu exterior.

Olho e comovo-me,
Comovo-me como a água corre quando o chão é inclinado,
E a minha poesia é natural como o levantar-se o vento ...

34) XVI

Quem me dera que a minha vida fosse um carro de bois
Que vem a chiar, manhãzinha cedo, pela estrada
E que para de onde veio volta depois
Quase à noitinha pela mesma estrada.

Eu não tinha que ter esperanças—tinha só que ter rodas ...   *5*
A minha velhice não tinha rugas nem cabelo branco ...
Quando eu já não servia, tiravam-me as rodas
E eu ficava virado e partido no fundo de um barranco.

35) XX

O Tejo é mais belo que o rio que corre pela minha aldeia,
Mas o Tejo não é mais belo que o rio que corre pela minha aldeia
Porque o Tejo não é o rio que corre pela minha aldeia.

O Tejo tem grandes navios
E navega nele ainda,   *5*
Para aqueles que vêem em tudo o que lá não está,
A memória das naus.

O Tejo desce de Espanha
E o Tejo entra no mar em Portugal.
Toda a gente sabe isso.   *10*
Mas poucos sabem qual é o rio da minha aldeia
E para onde ele vai
E donde ele vem.
E por isso, porque pertence a menos gente,
É mais livre e maior o rio da minha aldeia.   *over*   *15*

From THE KEEPER OF FLOCKS

33)   XIV

I don't care about rhyme. You seldom find
Two trees alike, standing side by side.
I think and write, just as flowers have colour,
But with less perfection in the way I express myself,
For I lack the godlike simplicity   *5*
Of being nothing but my outward self.

I look, and am moved,
Moved just as water flows where the ground slopes,
And my poetry comes as naturally as the wind rises . . .

34)   XVI

How I wish my life were an ox-cart
Squealing along the road in the early morning,
And going back later to where it came from,
By the same road, almost at dusk!

Then I wouldn't need hope—I would only need wheels . . .   *5*
My old age would mean neither white hair nor wrinkles . . .
When I was of no more use, they'd take my wheels off,
And I'd lie overturned and broken, down in some gully.

35)   XX

The Tagus is fairer than the river flowing through my village,
But the Tagus isn't fairer than the river flowing through my village
Because the Tagus isn't the river flowing through my village.

There are big ships on the Tagus
And, still sailing on it   *5*
For those who see in everything what isn't there,
Memories of the caravels.

The Tagus comes down from Spain
And the Tagus meets the sea in Portugal.
Everyone knows that.   *10*
But few know the name of my local river
Or where it goes
Or where it comes from.
And so, since it exists for fewer people,
My local river has more freedom and greatness.   *15*

Pelo Tejo vai-se para o Mundo.
Para além do Tejo há a América
E a fortuna daqueles que a encontram.
Ninguém nunca pensou no que há para além
Do rio da minha aldeia.   20

O rio da minha aldeia não faz pensar em nada.
Quem está ao pé dele está só ao pé dele.

36)   XXV

As bolas de sabão que esta criança
Se entretém a largar de uma palhinha
São translùcidamente uma filosofia toda.
Claras, inúteis e passageiras como a Natureza,
Amigas dos olhos como as cousas,   5
São aquilo que são
Com uma precisão redondinha e aérea,
E ninguém, nem mesmo a criança que as deixa,
Pretende que elas são mais do que parecem ser.

Algumas mal se vêem no ar lúcido.   10
São como a brisa que passa e mal toca nas flores
E que só sabemos que passa
Porque qualquer coisa se aligeira em nós
E aceita tudo mais nìtidamente.

37)   XXVI

Às vezes, em dias de luz perfeita e exacta,
Em que as coisas têm toda a realidade que podem ter,
Pergunto a mim próprio devagar
Porque sequer atribuo eu
Beleza às coisas.   5

Uma flor acaso tem beleza?
Tem beleza acaso um fruto?
Não: têm cor e forma
E existência apenas.
A beleza é o nome de qualquer coisa que não existe   10
Que eu dou às coisas em troca do agrado que me dão.
Não significa nada.
Então porque digo eu das coisas: são belas?   *over*

The Tagus is the highway to the World.
Beyond the Tagus lies America
And a fortune for those who find it.
No one has ever wondered what lies beyond
My local river.   *20*

My local river reminds you of nothing.
If you're beside it, you're beside it, that's all.

36)   XXV

The soap-bubbles which this child
Blows from a straw for amusement
Are transparently a philosophy in themselves.
Shiny, useless and transient as Nature,
Pleasing the eye as things do,   *5*
They are what they are
In a precisely spherical and airy way,
And no one, not even the child who launches them
Claims they are more than they seem.

There are some you can scarcely see in the clear air.   *10*
They're like the passing breeze which scarcely stirs the flowers,
Its passing known to us only
Because something quickens within us
And accepts all things with clearer insight.

37)   XXVI

Sometimes, on days of pure and perfect light,
When things are as real as real can be,
I quietly ask myself
Just what makes me suppose
That there is beauty in things.   *5*

Is there beauty in a flower, then?
Is there then beauty in a fruit?
No: they have colour and shape
And they exist, that's all.
Beauty is something non-existent, the name   *10*
I give to things in return for the pleasure they give me.
It has no meaning.
Why then do I say that things are beautiful?

Sim, mesmo a mim, que vivo só de viver,
Invisíveis, vêm ter comigo as mentiras dos homens   *15*
Perante as coisas,
Perante as coisas que simplesmente existem.

Que difícil ser próprio e não ver senão o visível!

38)   **XXXI**
Se às vezes digo que as flores sorriem
E se eu disser que os rios cantam,
Não é porque eu julgue que há sorrisos nas flores
E cantos no correr dos rios . . .
É porque assim faço mais sentir aos homens falsos   *5*
A existência verdadeiramente real das flores e dos rios.

Porque escrevo para eles me lerem sacrifico-me às vezes
À sua estupidez de sentidos . . .
Não concordo comigo mas absolvo-me,
Porque só sou essa coisa séria, um intérprete da Natureza,   *10*
Porque há homens que não percebem a sua linguagem,
Por ela não ser linguagem nenhuma.

39)   **XXXII**
Ontem à tarde um homem das cidades
Falava à porta da estalagem.
Falava comigo também.
Falava da justiça e da luta para haver justiça
E dos operários que sofrem,   *5*
E do trabalho constante, e dos que têm fome,
E dos ricos, que só têm costas para isso.

E, olhando para mim, viu-me lágrimas nos olhos
E sorriu com agrado, julgando que eu sentia
O ódio que ele sentia, e a compaixão   *10*
Que ele dizia que sentia.

(Mas eu mal o estava ouvindo.
Que me importam a mim os homens
E o que sofrem ou supõem que sofrem?
Sejam como eu—não sofrerão.   *over*   *15*

Yes, even to me, who live just by living,
Come all unseen the lies men tell   15
When faced with things,
When faced with things which simply exist.

How hard it is to be oneself and see only what is there!

38)   XXXI

If I sometimes say that flowers smile,
If I should ever say that rivers sing,
It's not because I fancy there are smiles in flowers
Or songs in rivers as they flow . . .
It's because in that way I bring home to men fond of lies   5
That flowers and rivers really and truly exist.

Because I want them to read what I write, I sometimes sacrifice
   myself
To their foolish feelings . . .
I know I'm wrong, but I have an excuse:
I'm seriously just this: an interpreter of Nature,   10
For there are men who don't understand her language,
Because it isn't a language at all.

39)   XXXII

Last evening a city-dweller
Was talking at the door of the inn.
He talked to me too.
He talked about justice and the struggle for justice,
The sufferings of the workers,   5
Unending toil, and those who go hungry,
And the rich, who just have to put up with it.

And when he looked at me, he saw tears in my eyes
And smiled with pleasure, for he thought that I felt
The hatred he felt, and the pity   10
He said he felt.

(But I scarcely heard a word he said.
What are men to me
And their sufferings, real or imagined?
Let them be like me: they won't suffer then.   15

Todo o mal do mundo vem de nos importarmos uns com os outros,
Quer para fazer bem, quer para fazer mal.
A nossa alma e o céu e a terra bastam-nos.
Querer mais é perder isto, e ser infeliz).

Eu no que estava pensando   20
Quando o amigo de gente falava
(E isso me comoveu até às lágrimas),
Era em como a murmúrio longínquo dos chocalhos
A esse entardecer
Não parecia os sinos duma capela pequenina   25
A que fossem à missa as flores e os regatos
E as almas simples como a minha.

(Louvado seja Deus que não sou bom,
E tenho o egoísmo natural das flores
E dos rios que seguem o seu caminho   30
Preocupados sem o saber
Só com florir e ir correndo.

É essa a única missão no mundo,
Essa—existir claramente,
E saber fazê-lo sem pensar nisso).   35

E o homem calara-se, olhando o poente.
Mas que tem com o poente quem odeia e ama?

40)   **XXXIV**
Acho tão natural que não se pense
Que me ponho a rir às vezes, sòzinho,
Não sei bem de quê, mas é de qualquer coisa
Que tem que ver com haver gente que pensa . . .

Que pensará o meu muro da minha sombra?   5
Pergunto-me às vezes isto até dar por mim
A perguntar-me coisas . . .
E então desagrado-me, e incomodo-me
Como se desse por mim com um pé dormente . . .

Que pensará isto de aquilo?   10
Nada pensa nada.
Terá a terra consciência das pedras e plantas que tem?
Se ela a tiver, que a tenha . . .   *over*

The whole trouble with the world is that we mind each other's
  business,
So as to do good or so as to do evil.
Our souls and heaven and earth are all we need:
To want more is to lose these and be unhappy).

What *I* was thinking about   20
While humanity's friend was talking
(And it was *that* moved me to tears),
  Was how it was that the distant murmur of cattle-bells
As evening came down
Was *not* like the bells of a tiny chapel   25
Where brooks and flowers attended Mass
Along with simple souls like mine.

(I'm not a good man—God be praised,
I'm instinctively selfish like the flowers
And rivers going their own sweet way   30
Unwittingly engaged
In flowering and in flowing and no more.

That's the only thing we're here for,
Just that: to exist clearly
And manage it without wondering how it's done).   35

The man had fallen silent as he looked at the sunset.
But what's the sunset to one who hates and loves?

40)   XXXIV
To me it seems so natural not to think
That sometimes I start laughing to myself
At what? I'm not quite sure, but something
To do with the idea of people thinking . . .

What will my wall think of my shadow?   5
That's what I sometimes wonder—till I notice
That I'm wondering,
And then I feel annoyed and ill at ease,
As if I found my foot had gone to sleep.

What will this think of that?   10
Nothing thinks at all.
Will the Earth ever know it has stones and plants?
If it does, then let it.

Que me importa isso a mim?
Se eu pensasse nessas coisas,   *15*
Deixaria de ver as árvores e as plantas
E deixava de ver a Terra,
Para ver só os meus pensamentos . . .
Entristecia e ficava às escuras.
E assim, sem pensar, tenho a Terra e o Céu.   *20*

41)   XXXIX
O mistério das coisas, onde está ele?
Onde está ele que não aparece
Pelo menos a mostrar-nos que é mistério?
Que sabe o rio disso e que sabe a árvore
E eu, que não sou mais do que eles, que sei disso?   *5*
Sempre que olho para as coisas e penso no que os homens pensam
    delas,
Rio como um regato que soa fresco numa pedra.

Porque o único sentido oculto das coisas
É elas não terem sentido oculto nenhum.
É mais estranho do que todas as estranhezas   *10*
E do que os sonhos de todos os poetas
E os pensamentos de todos os filósofos,
Que as coisas sejam realmente o que parecem ser
E não haja nada que compreender.

Sim, eis o que os meus sentidos aprenderam sòzinhos:—   *15*
As coisas não têm significação: têm existência.
As coisas são o único sentido oculto das coisas.

42)   XLIV
Acordo de noite sùbitamente,
E o meu relógio ocupa a noite toda.
Não sinto a Natureza lá fora.
O meu quarto é uma coisa escura com paredes vagamente
    brancas.
Lá fora há um sossego como se nada existisse.   *5*
Só o relógio prossegue o seu ruído.
E esta pequena coisa de engrenagens que está em cima da
    minha mesa
Abafa toda a existência da terra e do céu . . .
Quase que me perco a pensar o que isto significa,   *over*

What's that to me?
If I thought of things like that,   *15*
I'd stop seeing trees and plants
And I wouldn't see the Earth any more,
I'd only see what I was thinking.
I'd be depressed and at a loss.
So, with no thinking, Earth and Heaven are mine.   *20*

41)   XXXIX
Where is it, this mystery of things?
Where is it, and why doesn't it at least
Appear, and prove that it's a mystery?
What does a river know of this, what does a tree know,
And what do I know, who am no more than they?   *5*
Whenever I look at things and think of men's thoughts about
    them
I laugh like a brook coolly babbling over stones.

For the only hidden meaning of things
Is that they have no hidden meaning at all.
It's stranger than strangeness itself,   *10*
Stranger than the dreams of all poets
And the thoughts of all philosophers,
That things really are what they seem,
So that there's nothing to understand.

There! That's what my senses learned unaided:—   *15*
Things have no meaning: they have being.
Things are the only hidden meaning of things.

42)   XLIV
In the night I suddenly awake,
And my watch utterly pervades the night.
Nature out there is beyond my ken.
My room is something dark with dim white walls.
Outside is peace, as if nothing existed.   *5*
The watch alone still makes its noise.
And this little cluster of cogwheels, lying on my table,
Muffles the very existence of earth and heaven . . .
I almost forget myself and wonder what it means,

Mas estaco, e sinto-me sorrir na noite com os cantos da boca,   *10*
Porque a única coisa que o meu relógio simboliza ou significa
Enchendo com a sua pequenez a noite enorme
É a curiosa sensação de encher a noite enorme
Com a sua pequenez . . .

43)   XLVI

Deste modo ou daquele modo,
Conforme calha ou não calha,
Podendo às vezes dizer o que penso,
E outras vezes dizendo-o mal e com misturas,
Vou escrevendo os meus versos sem querer,   *5*
Como se escrever não fosse uma coisa feita de gestos,
Como se escrever fosse uma coisa que me acontecesse
Como dar-me o sol de fora.

Procuro dizer o que sinto
Sem pensar em que o sinto.   *10*
Procuro encostar as palavras à ideia
E não precisar dum corredor
Do pensamento para as palavras.

Nem sempre consigo sentir o que sei que devo sentir.
O meu pensamento só muito devagar atravessa o rio a nado   *15*
Porque lhe pesa o fato que os homens o fizeram usar.

Procuro despir-me do que aprendi,
Procuro esquecer-me do modo de lembrar que me ensinaram,
E raspar a tinta com que me pintaram os sentidos,
Desencaixotar as minhas emoções verdadeiras,
Desembrulhar-me e ser eu, não Alberto Caeiro,   *20*
Mas um animal humano que a Natureza produziu.

E assim escrevo, querendo sentir a Natureza, nem sequer como
    um homem,
Mas como quem sente a Natureza, e mais nada.
E assim escrevo, ora bem, ora mal,   *25*
Ora acertando com o que quero dizer, ora errando,
Caindo aqui, levantando-me acolá,
Mas indo sempre no meu caminho como um cego teimoso.

over

But I stop short, and find myself faintly smiling in the dark,   *10*
For the only thing my watch means or stands for,
As it fills the boundless night with its tiny self,
Is the odd feeling that it fills the boundless night
With its tiny self . . .

43)   XLVI
Somehow or other,
Getting it right or getting it wrong,
Able at times to say what I think,
And at others saying it badly and confusedly,
I write my poems without meaning to,   *5*
As though writing did not involve any action,
As though writing were something which happened to me,
Like the sun shining on me out of doors.

I try to say what I feel,
Without thinking about feeling it.   *10*
I try to bring the words and the ideas together
Without the need for a corridor
Leading from thought to word.

Sometimes I even fail to feel what I know I should feel.
My thought swims the river, but it's painfully slow,   *15*
For men have made it wear clothes which weigh it down.

I try to strip myself of what I have learned,
I try to forget what they taught me about remembering,
To scrape off the paint they coloured my senses with,
To unpack what I really feel,   *20*
To unwrap myself and be me, not Alberto Caeiro
But a human animal produced by Nature.

And so, wishing to feel Nature, I write, not even as a man,
But as one who feels Nature and nothing else.
And so I write, now well, now badly,   *25*
Now managing to say what I mean, now failing to,
Falling down here, picking myself up again there,
But still going my own way like a blind man on his mettle.

Ainda assim, sou alguém.
Sou o Descobridor da Natureza.
Sou o Argonauta das sensações verdadeiras.   *30*
Trago ao Universo um novo Universo
Porque trago ao Universo ele-próprio.

Isto sinto e isto escrevo
Perfeitamente sabedor e sem que não veja   *35*
Que são cinco horas do amanhecer
E que o sol, que ainda não mostrou a cabeça
Por cima do muro do horizonte,
Ainda assim já se lhe vêem as pontas dos dedos
Agarrando o cimo do muro   *40*
Do horizonte cheio de montes baixos.

From POEMAS INCONJUNTOS

44)   Ontem o pregador de verdades dele
       Falou outra vez comigo.
       Falou do sofrimento das classes que trabalham
       (Não do das pessoas que sofrem, que é afinal quem sofre).
       Falou da injustiça de uns terem dinheiro,   *5*
       E de outros terem fome, que não sei se é fome de comer,
       Ou se é só fome da sobremesa alheia.
       Falou de tudo quanto pudesse fazê-lo zangar-se.

       Que feliz deve ser quem pode pensar na infelicidade dos outros!
       Que estúpido se não sabe que a infelicidade dos outros é deles,   *10*
       E não se cura de fora,
       Porque sofrer não é ter falta de tinta
       Ou o caixote não ter aros de ferro!

       Haver injustiça é como haver morte.
       Eu nunca daria um passo para alterar   *15*
       Aquilo a que chamam a injustiça do mundo.
       Mil passos que desse para isso
       Eram só mil passos.
       Aceito a injustiça como aceito uma pedra não ser redonda,
       E um sobreiro não ter nascido pinheiro ou carvalho.   *20*

       Cortei a laranja em duas, e as duas partes não podiam ficar iguais.
       Para qual fui injusto—eu, que as vou comer a ambas?

Even so, I'm somebody.
I'm the Discoverer of Nature.   30
I'm the Argonaut of true feeling.
I bring to the Universe a new Universe,
For to the Universe I bring—itself.

This I feel and this I write,
In perfect awareness and not failing to see   35
That it's five o'clock in the morning
And that the sun has not yet shown its head
Above the wall of the horizon,
Though its finger-tips can already be seen
Gripping the top of the wall   40
Of the horizon with its line of low hills.

From SPORADIC POEMS

44)   Yesterday the preacher of personal truths
       Talked to me once more.
       He talked about the sufferings of the working classes
       (Not the individuals who suffer—the ones who *really* suffer).
       He said how unjust it is that some should have money   5
       While others are hungry; but did he mean hungry for food
       Or only hungry for someone else's dessert?

       He talked about anything that could make him angry.
       How happy the man must be who can think of other people's
           unhappiness!
       And how stupid not to know that their unhappiness is for *them*, 10
       And cannot be cured from outside,
       For suffering isn't like running out of ink
       Or having a trunk that isn't bound with iron!

       There is injustice, the same as there is death.
       I wouldn't walk a single step to change   15
       What's known as the injustice of the world.
       If I walked a thousand steps for that
       They would only be a thousand steps.
       I accept injustice as I accept that stones may not be round
       And that cork-trees weren't born to be pines or oaks.   20

       I cut the orange in two, and couldn't make the two parts equal.
       To which was I unjust? I'm going to eat them both!

⅄ 45)   A espantosa realidade das coisas
         É a minha descoberta de todos os dias.
         Cada coisa é o que é,
         E é difícil explicar a alguém quanto isso me alegra,
         E quanto isso me basta.   5

         Basta existir para se ser completo.

         Tenho escrito bastantes poemas.
         Hei-de escrever muitos mais, naturalmente.
         Cada poema meu diz isto,
         E todos os meus poemas são diferentes,   10
         Porque cada coisa que há é uma maneira de dizer isto.

         Às vezes ponho-me a olhar para uma pedra.
         Não me ponho a pensar se ela sente.
         Não me perco a chamar-lhe minha irmã.
         Mas gosto dela por ela ser uma pedra,   15
         Gosto dela porque ela não sente nada,
         Gosto dela porque ela não tem parentesco nenhum comigo.

         Outras vezes oiço passar o vento,
         E acho que só para ouvir passar o vento vale a pena ter nascido.

         Eu não sei o que é que os outros pensarão lendo isto;   20
         Mas acho que isto deve estar bem porque o penso sem esforço,
         Nem ideia de outras pessoas a ouvir-me pensar;
         Porque o penso sem pensamentos,
         Porque o digo como as minhas palavras o dizem.

         Uma vez chamaram-me poeta materialista,   25
         E eu admirei-me, porque não julgava
         Que se me pudesse chamar qualquer coisa.
         Eu nem sequer sou poeta: vejo.
         Se o que escrevo tem valor, não sou eu que o tenho:
         O valor está ali, nos meus versos.   30
         Tudo isso é absolutamente independente da minha vontade.

46)   Quando vier a primavera,
         Se eu já estiver morto,
         As flores florirão da mesma maneira
         E as árvores não serão menos verdes que na primavera passada.
         A realidade não precisa de mim.   *over*   5

45) The astonishing reality of things
      Is something I discover every day.
      Each thing is what it is,
      And it's hard to explain how glad this makes me,
      And how content.   5

      To be fulfilled, existence is enough.

      I've written several poems.
      No doubt I shall write many more.
      Each of my poems says this,
      And all my poems are different,   10
      Because each thing that exists is one way of saying this.

      Sometimes I start looking at a stone.
      I don't start wondering if it feels.
      I don't waste time calling it my brother.
      But I like it because it's a stone.   15
      I like it because it feels nothing.
      I like it because we're in no way related.

      At other times I hear the wind blowing,
      And I feel that just to hear the wind blowing is reason enough
         for being born.

      I don't know what others will think when they read this; 20
      But I feel this must be good because I think it effortlessly,
      Without caring whether others hear me think;
      Because I think it unthinkingly,
      Because I say it the way my words say it.

      They once called me a materialist poet.   25
      I was surprised, because I didn't suppose
      I could be called anything.
      I'm not even a poet: I *see.*
      If what I write has some value, that value isn't mine:
      It lies there, in my verse.   30
      It's all utterly independent of my will.

46) When spring comes round,
      If I should be dead,
      Flowers will bloom just the same,
      And trees will be no less green than they were last spring.
      Reality doesn't need me.   5

Sinto uma alegria enorme
Ao pensar que a minha morte não tem importância nenhuma.

Se soubesse que amanhã morria
E a primavera era depois de amanhã,
Morreria contente, porque ela era depois de amanhã.   *10*
Se esse é o seu tempo, quando havia ela de vir senão no seu
    tempo?
Gosto que tudo seja real e que tudo esteja certo;
E gosto porque assim seria, mesmo que eu não gostasse.
Por isso, se morrer agora, morro contente,
Porque tudo é real e tudo está certo.   *15*

Podem rezar latim sobre o meu caixão, se quiserem.
Se quiserem, podem dançar e cantar à roda dele.
Não tenho preferências para quando já não puder ter preferências.
O que for, quando for, é que será o que é.

47) Se eu morrer novo,
Sem poder publicar livro nenhum,
Sem ver a cara que têm os meus versos em letra impressa
Peço que, se se quiserem ralar por minha causa,
Que não se ralem.   *5*
Se assim aconteceu, assim está certo.

Mesmo que os meus versos nunca sejam impressos,
Eles lá terão a sua beleza, se forem belos.
Mas eles não podem ser belos e ficar por imprimir,
Porque as raízes podem estar debaixo da terra   *10*
Mas as flores florescem ao ar livre e à vista.
Tem que ser assim por força. Nada o pode impedir.

Se eu morrer muito novo, oiçam isto:
Nunca fui senão uma criança que brincava.
Fui gentio como o sol e a água,   *15*
De uma religião universal que só os homens não têm.
Fui feliz porque não pedi coisa nenhuma,
Nem procurei achar nada,
Nem achei que houvesse mais explicação
Que a palavra explicação não ter sentido nenhum.   *20*

over

I feel boundless joy
To think that my death simply doesn't matter.

If I knew I was to die tomorrow,
And spring was to be the day after,
I'd die content that it was to be the day after.   *10*
If that's the time for it, when should it come, if not then?
I like everything to be real and everything to be right.
I like things that way because they'd be the same even if I didn't.
And so, if I die now, I die content,
Because everything's real and everything's right.   *15*

They can say Latin prayers over my coffin, if they like.
If they like, they can sing and dance around it.
I've no preferences for the time when I can no longer have any.
Whatever comes, whenever it comes, will be what it is.

47)   If I die young,
Without publishing a single book,
Without seeing what my verse looks like in print,
In case you should feel like worrying about me
Please don't.   *5*
If that's the way it happened, it's right that way.

Even if my verse is never printed,
It will have a beauty of its own, so far as it's beautiful.
But it cannot be beautiful and remain unprinted,
Because though the roots may be underground,   *10*
The flowers bloom in the open, in full view.
It must be so, perforce. Nothing can prevent it.

If I die very young, let me tell you this:
I was never more than a child at play.
I was as pagan as sun and water,   *15*
With a universal religion unknown to man alone.
I was happy because I asked for nothing,
Nor tried to find anything,
Nor found there was any more explanation for things
Than that the word 'explanation' is meaningless.   *20*

Não desejei senão estar ao sol ou à chuva—
Ao sol quando havia sol
E à chuva quando estava chovendo
(E nunca a outra coisa),
Sentir calor e frio e vento,   *25*
E não ir mais longe.

Uma vez amei, julguei que me amariam,
Mas não fui amado.
Não fui amado pela única grande razão—
Porque não tinha que ser.   *30*

Consolei-me voltando ao sol e à chuva,
E sentando-me outra vez à porta de casa.
Os campos, afinal, não são tão verdes para os que são amados
Como para os que o não são.
Sentir é estar distraído.   *35*

48) É noite. A noite é muito escura. Numa casa a uma grande
         distância
      Brilha a luz duma janela.
      Vejo-a, e sinto-me humano dos pés à cabeça.
      É curioso que toda a vida do indivíduo que ali mora, e que não
         sei quem é,
      Atrai-me só por essa luz vista de longe.   *5*
      Sem dúvida que a vida dele é real e ele tem cara, gestos, família
         e profissão.
      Mas agora só me importa a luz da janela dele.
      Apesar de a luz estar ali por ele a ter acendido,
      A luz é a realidade imediata para mim.
      Eu nunca passo para além da realidade imediata.   *10*
      Para além de realidade imediata não há nada.
      Se eu, de onde estou, só vejo aquela luz,
      Em relação à distância onde estou há só aquela luz.
      O homem e a família dele são reais do lado de lá da janela.
      Eu estou do lado de cá, a uma grande distância.   *15*
      A luz apagou-se.
      Que me importa que o homem continue a existir?

All I wanted was to be in sunshine or rain—
In sunshine when the sun shone
And in rain when it was raining
(And never in anything else),
To feel the heat, the cold, the wind,   *25*
And go no further.

I once loved, I thought I would be loved
But I wasn't loved.
I wasn't loved for the only reason that matters—
It was not to be.   *30*

I found comfort in going back to sunshine and rain,
And sitting down once more at the house-door.
The fields, after all, are not so green for those who are loved
As they are for those who are not.
Feelings are a distraction.   *35*

48) It's night: a very dark night. In a house a long way off
A lighted window shines.
I see it and feel human from head to foot.
It's strange how the whole life of the one who lives there—
    I don't know who—
Draws me with just that light seen from afar.   *5*
No doubt his life is real: he has a face, gestures, a family,
    a profession.
But now all I care about is the light in his window.
Although the light is there because he lit it,
That light is immediate reality to me.
I never go beyond immediate reality.   *10*
Beyond immediate reality lies nothing.
If I, from where I am, see only that light,
That light is all there is for me, far away as I am.
The man and his family are real on the other side of the window.
I'm on this side of it, a long way off.   *15*
Now the light goes out.
What do I care if the man goes on existing?

49)   Vive, dizes, no presente;
Vive só no presente.

Mas eu não quero o presente, quero a realidade;
Quero as coisas que existem, não o tempo que as mede.

O que é o presente?   5
É uma coisa relativa ao passado e ao futuro.
É uma coisa que existe em virtude de outras coisas existirem.
Eu quero só a realidade, as coisas sem presente.

Não quero incluir o tempo no meu esquema.
Não quero pensar nas coisas como presentes; quero pensar
    nelas como coisas.   10
Não quero separá-las de si-próprias, tratando-as por presentes.

Eu nem por reais as devia tratar.
Eu não as devia tratar por nada.

Eu devia vê-las, apenas vê-las;
Vê-las até não poder pensar nelas,   15
Vê-las sem tempo, nem espaço,
Ver podendo dispensar tudo menos o que se vê.
É esta a ciência de ver, que não é nenhuma.

49) 'Live in the present', you say,
      'Live only in the present'.

      But I don't want the present: I want reality;
      I want what exists, not the time which measures it.

      What is the present?   *5*
      It's something relative to past and future.
      It's something that exists because there are other things that
         exist.
      I just want reality, things with no present.

      I don't want time in my purview at all.
      I don't want to think of things as present: I want to think of
         them as things.   *10*
      I don't want to separate them from themselves by regarding
         them as present.

      I ought not even to regard them as real.
      I ought not to regard them as anything.

      I ought to see them, only see them,
      See them till I cannot think of them,   *15*
      See them divorced from time and space,
      See with the help of nothing but that which can be seen.
      That's the science of seeing—no science at all.

      END OF *Caeiro*

50) Vem sentar-te comigo, Lídia, à beira do rio.
Sossegadamente fitemos o seu curso e aprendamos
Que a vida passa, e não estamos de mãos enlaçadas.
(Enlacemos as mãos).

Depois pensemos, crianças adultas, que a vida   *5*
Passa e não fica, nada deixa e nunca regressa,
Vai para um mar muito longe, para ao pé do Fado,
Mais longe que os deuses.

Desenlacemos as mãos, porque não vale a pena cansarmo-nos.
Quer gozemos, quer não gozemos, passamos como o rio.   *10*
Mais vale saber passar silenciosamente
E sem desassossêgos grandes.

Sem amores, nem ódios, nem paixões que levantam a voz,
Nem invejas que dão movimento demais aos olhos,
Nem cuidados, porque se os tivesse o rio sempre correria,   *15*
E sempre iria ter ao mar.

Amemo-nos tranquilamente, pensando que podíamos,
Se quiséssemos, trocar beijos e abraços e carícias,
Mas que mais vale estarmos sentados ao pé um do outro
Ouvindo correr o rio e vendo-o.   *20*

Colhamos flores, pega tu nelas e deixa-as
No colo, e que o seu perfume suavize o momento—
Este momento em que sossegadamente não cremos em nada,
Pagãos inocentes da decadência.

Ao menos, se for sombra antes, lembrar-te-ás de mim depois   *25*
Sem que a minha lembrança te arda ou te fira ou te mova,
Porque nunca enlaçamos as mãos, nem nos beijamos
Nem fomos mais do que crianças.

E se antes do que eu levares o óbolo ao barqueiro sombrio,
Eu nada terei que sofrer ao lembrar-me de ti.   *30*
Ser-me-ás suave à memória lembrando-te assim—à beira-rio,
Pagã triste e com flores no regaço.

50) Come sit by my side, Lydia, on the bank of the river.
Calmly let us watch it flow, and learn
That life passes, and we are not holding hands.
(Let us hold hands).

Then let us reflect as grown-up children, that life   5
Passes and does not stay, leaves nothing, never returns,
Goes to a sea far away, near to Fate itself,
Further than the gods.

Let us hold hands no more: why should we tire ourselves?
For our pleasure, for our pain, we pass on like the river.   10
'Tis better to know how to pass on silently,
With no great disquiet.

With neither loves nor hates, nor passions raising their voice,
Nor envies making the eye rove too restlessly,
Nor cares, for if it knew care the river would flow no less,   15
Would still join the sea in the end.

Let us love each other calmly, with the thought that we could,
If we chose, freely kiss and caress and embrace,
But that we do better to be seated side by side
Hearing the river flow, and seeing it.   20

Let us gather flowers, and do you take some and leave them
In your lap, and let their scent lend sweetness to the moment—
This moment when calmly we believe in nothing,
Innocent pagans of the decadence.

At least, should I first become a shade, you will remember
    me after,   25
Though, remembered, I may not inflame nor hurt nor disturb you,
For we never hold hands, nor kiss,
Nor were we ever more than children.

And if, before me, you take the obol to the gloomy boatman,
I shall have no cause to suffer when I remember you.   30
You will be sweet to my memory if I remember you thus, on
    the river bank,
A sorrowful pagan maid, with flowers in her lap.

51) Só esta liberdade nos concedem
      Os deuses: submetermo-nos
      Ao seu domínio por vontade nossa.
      Mais vale assim fazermos
      Porque só na ilusão da liberdade   5
      A liberdade existe.

      Nem outro jeito os deuses, sobre quem
      O eterno fado pesa,
      Usam para seu calmo e possuído
      Convencimento antigo   10
      De que é divina e livre a sua vida.

      Nós, imitando os deuses,
      Tão pouco livres como eles no Olimpo,
      Como quem pela areia
      Ergue castelos para encher os olhos,   15
      Ergamos nossa vida
      E os deuses saberão agradecer-nos
      O sermos tão como eles.

52) Vós que, crentes em Cristos e Marias,
      Turvais da minha fonte as claras águas
      Só para me dizerdes
      Que há águas de outra espécie

      Banhando prados com melhores horas,—   5
      Dessas outras regiões pra que falar-me
      Se estas águas e prados
      São de aqui e me agradam?

      Esta realidade os deuses deram
      E para bem real a deram externa.   10
      Que serão os meus sonhos
      Mais que a obra dos deuses?

      Deixai-me a Realidade do momento
      E os meus deuses tranquilos e imediatos
      Que não moram no Vago   15
      Mas nos campos e rios.   *over*

51) In this respect alone the gods allow us
To be free: they let us of our own accord
Acknowledge them our masters.
We do well to act thus,
For in the illusion of being free   *5*
Alone lies freedom.

Just so the gods, themselves
The victims of eternal fate,
Are able to maintain, serenely self-possessed,
Their age-old conviction   *10*
That theirs is a life divine and free.

No more free than the gods on Olympus,
Let us follow their example
And, just as on sand one might set up
A castle to impress the eye,   *15*
Let us set up our lives.
The gods will surely thank us
For being so much like them.

52) Ye who believing in Christs and in Marys
Trouble the limpid waters of my spring
Merely to tell me
That there are waters of another kind

Bathing meadows in better times,—   *5*
Why speak to me of those other regions
If these waters, these meadows
Are of here and now and delight me?

This reality the gods bestowed,
And made it outward that it might be real indeed.   *10*
What more can my dreams be
Than the work of the gods?

Leave me the Reality of the moment
And my quiet and immediate gods
Who dwell not in Vagueness   *15*
But in fields and rivers.

Deixai-me a vida ir-se pagãmente
Acompanhada plas avenas ténues
Com que os juncos das margens
Se confessam de Pã.   20

Vivei nos vossos sonhos e deixai-me
O altar imortal onde é meu culto
E a visível presença
Dos meus próximos deuses.

Inúteis procos do melhor que a vida,   25
Deixai a vida aos crentes mais antigos
Que a Cristo e a sua cruz
E Maria chorando.

Ceres, dona dos campos, me console
E Apolo e Vénus, e Urano antigo
E os trovões, com o interesse   30
De irem da mão de Jove.

53) Prefiro rosas, meu amor, à pátria,
E antes magnólias amo
Que a glória e a virtude.

Logo que a vida me não canse, deixo
Que a vida por mim passe
Logo que eu fique o mesmo.   5

Que importa àquele a quem já nada importa
Que um perca e outro vença,
Se a aurora raia sempre,

Se cada ano com a Primavera   10
As folhas aparecem
E com o Outono cessam?

E o resto, as outras coisas que os humanos
Acrescentam à vida,
Que me aumentam na alma?   15

Nada, salvo o desejo de indif'rença
E a confiança mole
Na hora fugitiva.

Let life pass for me in pagan mode
To the tune of the slender pipes
With which the reed-banks
Acknowledge Pan their god.   20

Live in your dreams and leave me
The undying altar where I worship,
And the visible presence
Of my nearest gods.

Ye who vainly woo what is better than life,   25
Leave life to believers in older things
Than Christ and his cross,
And Mary weeping.

Ceres, mistress of the fields, be my comfort,
Apollo and Venus too, and aged Uranus,   30
And the thunderbolts which fascinate
By coming from the hand of Jove.

53)   I prefer roses to my country,
And I love magnolias more,
Beloved, than glory or virtue.

So long as life does not weary me,
I give it leave to pass me by,   5
So long as I remain the same.

He who no longer knows care, what cares he
That one should win, another lose,
If dawn breaks nonetheless,

If every year when spring returns   10
The leaves unfold
And die with autumn-tide?

What of the rest, those other things
With which men supplement this life,
What do they add to my soul?   15

Nothing, save a wish for unconcern,
And soft surrender
To the fleeting hour.

54) Segue o teu destino,
      Rega as tuas plantas,
      Ama as tuas rosas.
      O resto é a sombra
      De árvores alheias.   *5*

      A realidade
      Sempre é mais ou menos
      Do que nós queremos.
      Só nós somos sempre
      Iguais a nós-próprios.   *10*

      Suave é viver só.
      Grande e nobre é sempre
      Viver simplesmente.
      Deixa a dor nas aras
      Como ex-voto aos deuses.   *15*

      Vê de longe a vida.
      Nunca a interrogues.
      Ela nada pode
      Dizer-te. A resposta
      Está além dos deuses.   *20*

      Mas serenamente
      Imita o Olimpo
      No teu coração.
      Os deuses são deuses
      Porque não se pensam.   *25*

55) Feliz aquele a quem a vida grata
      Concedeu que dos deuses se lembrasse
      E visse como eles
      Estas terrenas coisas onde mora
      Um reflexo mortal da imortal vida.   *5*
      Feliz, que quando a hora tributária
      Transpor seu átrio porque a Parca corte
      O fio fiado até ao fim,
      Gozar poderá o alto prémio
      De errar no Averno grato abrigo   *10*
      Da convivência.   *over*

54) Follow your fate,
        Water your plants,
        Love your roses.
        All else is the shade
        Of trees not your own.   *5*

        Reality
        Is always more, or less,
        Than we expect of it.
        We alone are always
        Equal to ourselves.   *10*

        'Tis sweet merely to live.
        'Tis always great and noble
        Simply to live.
        Leave sorrow on the altars
        As an offering to the gods.   *15*

        View life from afar.
        Ask it no questions.
        It can tell you
        Nothing. The answer
        Lies beyond the gods.   *20*

        But serenely
        Imitate Olympus
        Within your heart.
        The gods are gods because
        They never think of being.   *25*

55) Happy is he whom pleasant life
        Permitted to be mindful of the gods,
        To see as they do
        These earthly things where dwells
        A mortal reflex of a life immortal: *5*
        Happy, for when the tributary hour
        Crosses his threshold, Fate having cut
        The thread spun to its end,
        He will enjoy the high reward
        Of roaming in Avernus, pleasant abode   *10*
        Of good-fellowship.

Mas aquele que quer Cristo antepor
Aos mais antigos Deuses que no Olimpo
Seguiram a Saturno—
O seu blasfemo ser abandonado   *15*
Na fria expiação—até que os Deuses
De quem se esqueceu deles se recordem—
Erra, sombra inquieta, incertamente,
Nem a viúva lhe põe na boca
O óbolo a Caronte grato,   *20*
E sobre o seu corpo insepulto
Não deita terra o viandante.

56) Melhor destino que o de conhecer-se
Não frui quem mente frui. Antes, sabendo
Ser nada, que ignorando:
Nada dentro de nada.
Se não houver em mim poder que vença   *5*
As Parcas três e as moles do futuro,
Já me dêem os deuses
O poder de sabê-lo;
E a beleza, incriável por meu sestro,
Eu goze externa e dada, repetida   *10*
Em meus passivos olhos,
Lagos que a morte seca.

57) Como se cada beijo
Fora de despedida,
Minha Cloe, beijemo-nos, amando.
Talvez que já nos toque
No ombro a mão, que chama   *5*
À barca que não vem senão vazia;
E que no mesmo feixe
Ata o que mútuos fomos
E a alheia soma universal da vida.

58) O sono é bom pois despertamos dele
Para saber que é bom. Se a morte é sono
Despertaremos dela;
Se não, e não é sono,   *over*

But he who would set Christ above
The oldest Gods who on Olympus
Succeeded Saturn—
His blasphemous self, abandoned   15
To chill expiation—till the Gods
Remember him who forgot them—
Roams in uncertainty, an unquiet shade:
No widow places in his mouth
The obol pleasing to Charon,   20
Nor on his unburied corpse
Does the wayfarer scatter earth.

56) What finer fate can he enjoy who has a mind
Than know himself? Better to be nothing
Knowingly, than in ignorance—
Nothing twice over.
If I lack the power to overcome   5
The Fatal Sisters and the future's daunting mass,
May the gods give me at least
The power to know I lack it;
And may that beauty I am doomed not to create
Delight me as a gift awarded from without,   10
Reflected in my passive eyes,
Pools which death must drain.

57) As though each kiss
Were in farewell
Let us, O Chloe, kiss lovingly.
Perhaps already on our shoulders
Falls the hand that summons   5
To the ferry ever empty when it comes;
The hand that in the same sheaf
Binds what we were to each other
And the sum of all other lives.

58) Sleep is good, for when we awake
We discover its goodness. If death be sleep
We shall awake;
If we do not, and it be not sleep,

Conquanto em nós é nosso a refusemos   5
Enquanto em nossos corpos condenados
Dura, do carcereiro,
A licença indecisa.

Lídia, a vida mais vil antes que a morte,
Que desconheço, quero; e as flores colho   10
Que te entrego, votivas
De um pequeno destino.

59) Pesa o decreto atroz do fim certeiro.
Pesa a sentença igual do juiz ignoto
Em cada cerviz néscia. É entrudo e riem.
Felizes, porque neles pensa e sente
A vida, que não eles!   5

Se a ciência é vida, sábio é só o néscio.
Quão pouca diferença a mente interna
Do homem da dos brutos! Sus! Deixai
Brincar os moribundos!

De rosas, inda que de falsas teçam   10
Capelas veras. Breve e vão é o tempo
Que lhes é dado, e por misericórdia
Breve nem vão sentido.

60) Tudo que cessa é morte, e a morte é nossa
Se é para nós que cessa. Aquele arbusto
Fenece, e vai com ele
Parte da minha vida.
Em tudo quanto olhei fiquei em parte.   5
Com tudo quanto vi, se passa, passo,
Nem distingue a memória
O que vi do que fui.

61) Nem da erva humilde se o Destino esquece,
Saiba a lei o que vive.
De sua natureza murcham rosas
E prazeres se acabam.
Quem nos conhece, amigo, tais quais fomos?   5
Nem nós os conhecemos.

With all that in us lies let us have none of it,   5
As long as the jailor's lease
For our doomed bodies
Precariously endures.

The meanest life, O Lydia, I prefer
To unknown death, and I pluck these flowers   10
For you, the offerings
Of a minor destiny.

59)   Heavy the harsh decree of certain death,
Heavy the unknown judge's equal doom
On each unwitting head. The revellers laugh,
Happy because not they, but life
Within them thinks and feels!   5

If knowledge be life, the fool alone is wise.
The inner mind of man and that of beast—
How like each other! Come then, leave
The dying to their sport!

Though with false roses, let them weave   10
True garlands. Brief and vain the span
To them assigned, mercifully
Not felt as vain or brief.

60)   All things that end are death, and death is ours
If they should end for us. That bush
Withers and with it goes
Part of my life.
I remained in part in all I witnessed.   5
Involved in all I saw, I pass on when it passes,
And what I saw and what I was,
Remembered, are the same.

61)   If Fate does not forget the humble blade of grass,
Whatever lives must recognize the law.
By their nature roses fade
And pleasures terminate.
Who knows us, friend, just as we were?   5
Not even we know now.

62)   A cada qual, como a statura, é dada
       A justiça: uns faz altos
       O fado, outros felizes.
       Nada é prémio: sucede o que acontece.
       Nada, Lídia, devemos   5
       Ao fado, senão tê-lo.

63)   Se recordo quem fui, outrem me vejo,
       E o passado é o presente na lembrança.
       Quem fui é alguém que amo
       Porém sòmente em sonho.
       E a saudade que me aflige a mente   5
       Não é de mim nem do passado visto,
       Senão de quem habito
       Por trás dos olhos cegos.
       Nada, senão o instante, me conhece.
       Minha mesma lembrança é nada, e sinto   10
       Que quem sou e quem fui
       São sonhos diferentes.

64)   Não só quem nos odeia ou nos inveja
       Nos limita e oprime; quem nos ama
       Não menos nos limita.
       Que os deuses me concedam que, despido
       De afectos, tenha a fria liberdade   5
       Dos píncaros sem nada.
       Quem quer pouco, tem tudo; quem quer nada
       É livre; quem não tem, e não deseja,
       Homem, é igual aos deuses.

65)   Não sei se é amor que tens, ou amor que finges,
       O que me dás. Dás-mo. Tanto me basta.
       Já que o não sou por tempo,
       Seja eu jovem por erro.
       Pouco os deuses nos dão, e o pouco é falso.   5
       Porém, se o dão, falso que seja, a dádiva
       É verdadeira. Aceito,
       Cerro olhos: é bastante.
       Que mais quero?

62) Justice is meted out to each
Like height: fate makes some tall,
Others it makes happy.
No meed what comes, 'tis merely what befalls.
To fate we owe nothing, Lydia,   *5*
Save to be fated.

63) Recalling who I was, I see another self:
The past becomes the present in my memory.
The one I was is one I love,
Though only in a dream.
And the longing which troubles my spirit   *5*
Is not for me, nor for the witnessed past,
But for the one I dwell in
Behind unseeing eyes.
Nothing knows me, save the moment.
My memory itself a void, I feel   *10*
That who I am and who I was
Are different dreams.

64) Not only with their hatred or their envy
Do others limit and oppress us: by loving us
They limit us no less.
May the gods grant me, released
From all feeling, the chill freedom   *5*
Of barren mountain peaks.
He who wants little has all things; he who wants nothing
Is free; he who neither has nor desires,
A man, can match the gods.

65) This thing you give me, is it love you feel,
Or love you feign? You give it: that suffices me.
Though in years no novice,
Let me be one in delusion.
The gods give us little, and that little is false.   *5*
Yet, if they give it, for all its falseness
The gift is real. I take it
And close my eyes: 'tis enough.
Why ask for more?

66)   Do que quero renego, se o querê-lo
       Me pesa na vontade. Nada que haja
       Vale que lhe concedamos
       Uma atenção que doa.
       Meu balde exponho à chuva, por ter água.   5
       Minha vontade, assim, ao mundo exponho,
       Recebo o que me é dado,
       E o que falta não quero.

       O que me é dado quero
       Depois de dado, grato.   10

       Nem quero mais que o dado
       Ou que o tido desejo.

67)   Súbdito inútil de astros dominantes,
       Passageiros como eu, vivo uma vida
       Que não quero nem amo,
       Minha porque sou ela.

       No ergástulo de ser quem sou, contudo,   5
       De em mim pensar me livro, olhando no alto
       Os astros que dominam
       Submissos de os ver brilhar.

       Vastidão vã que finge de infinito
       (Como se o infinito se pudesse ver!)—   10
       Dá-me ela a liberdade?
       Como, se ela a não tem?

68)   Para os deuses as coisas são mais coisas.
       Não mais longe eles vêem, mas mais claro
       Na certa Natureza
       E a contornada vida . . .
       Não no vago que mal vêem   5
       Orla misteriosamente os seres,
       Mas nos detalhes claros
       Estão seus olhos.
       A Natureza é só uma superfície.
       Na sua superfície ela é profunda   10
       E tudo contém muito
       Se os olhos bem olharem.   *over*

66) I renounce what I want, if wanting it
Burdens my will. Nothing in existence
Warrants our heed
If heeding hurts.
To catch rain-water I leave my pitcher out.   *5*
Just so out in the world I leave my will.
I receive what I am given:
The rest I do not want.

What I am given I want, gratefully,
After the gift has been made.   *10*

No more than is given do I want:
I desire no more than is received.

67) A worthless vassal ruled by stars
Themselves as transient, I live a life
I neither want nor love,
Mine because I am one with it.

Yet in the dungeon of being what I am   *5*
I rid my thoughts of self by looking up
At the stars which rule
Those resigned to their radiance.

Inane immenseness feigning infinity
(As if the infinite could be seen!)—   *10*
Does it give me freedom?
What if it have none to give?

68) To the gods, things are more truly things.
No further, yet more clearly do they see
Nature's certainty
And life's definition . . .
Not the vagueness scarcely seen   *5*
Darkly describing the bounds of beings,
But the clear detail
Holds their gaze.
Nature is naught but surface.
In its surface it goes deep   *10*
And in all things there is much
For the observant eye.

Aprende, pois, tu, das cristãs angústias,
Ó traidor à multíplice presença
Dos deuses, a não teres   *15*
Véus nos olhos nem na alma.

69)   Aos deuses peço só que me concedam
O nada lhes pedir. A dita é um jugo
E o ser feliz oprime
Porque é um certo estado.
Não quieto nem inquieto meu ser calmo   *5*
Quero erguer alto acima de onde os homens
Têm prazer ou dores.

70)   Meu gesto que destrói
A mole das formigas,
Tomá-lo-ão elas por de um ser divino;
Mas eu não sou divino para mim.

Assim talvez os deuses   *5*
Para si o não sejam,
E só de serem do que nós maiores
Tirem o serem deuses para nós.

Seja qual for o certo,
Mesmo para com esses
Que cremos serem deuses, não sejamos   *10*
Inteiros numa fé talvez sem causa.

Learn, then, thou who feelest Christian pangs,
Thou traitor to the manifold presence
Of the gods, to brook no veil   15
Before thy eyes, nor before thy soul.

69)   All I ask of the gods is that they allow me
To ask them for nothing. Good fortune is a yoke,
And happiness a tyrant
By dint of being positive.
Neither troubled nor untroubled let me raise   5
My tranquil being high above the realms
Where men know pleasure or pain.

70)   My act when I destroy
The structure ants have raised,
Must seem to them divine indeed,
Yet in my own eyes I am not divine.

Perhaps, just so, the gods   5
No gods in their own eyes,
Merely because they are greater than we,
Appear as gods in ours.

Be the truth as it may,
Even towards those   10
Whom we consider gods, let us not be
Perfect in a faith which may be groundless.

END OF *Reis*

Notes

FERNANDO PESSOA

1. Composed in 1913, and originally published in *Renascença* no.
    1, February 1914, together with *Paùis* ('Quagmires'), under
    the heading 'Twilight Impressions', *Ó sino da minha aldeia*
    was subsequently republished in *Athena* no. 3, December
    1924. In a letter to João Gaspar Simões, dated 11 December
    1931, Pessoa explained that the 'village' where he was born
    was in fact a square in Lisbon, the Largo de São Carlos, and
    that the church bell in question was that of the 'Mártires' in
    the Chiado, another Lisbon square.

2. Written in 1914, first published in *Terra Nossa* no. 3, September
    1916, and republished in *Athena* no. 3, December 1924. The
    reader familiar with Wordsworth's poem 'The Reaper' will
    recognize its source. 'Reaping and singing' in Wordsworth's
    poem is echoed by 'Sings and reaps' in Pessoa's; 'The maiden
    sang/As if her song could have no ending' may have suggested
    'she sings as if' in l.11; and '*single* in the field,/Yon *solitary*
    Highland Lass' may account for 'loneliness' in l.4. Apart
    from these superficial points of contact, however, the two
    poems move in very different directions, and have a very
    different emphasis. Wordsworth's poem is richer in imagery;
    both are rich in suggestion, but Pessoa's ends on a note of un-
    fulfilled longing which is completely lacking in the English
    poem. When on 19 January 1915 Pessoa sent his famous letter
    to Armando Cortes-Rodrigues, he accompanied it with an
    earlier version of this poem, and this version has been pre-
    served. It contains two additional stanzas, occurring between
    stanzas 3 and 4, and 4 and 5 of the published version. L.14
    originally read *O que em mim ouve esta chorando* 'My hearing
    turns to tears'—a line less memorable than the one which

replaced it.

4. *joyful loneliness*. There is a definite oxymoron in the original, since *viuvez* means literally 'widowhood' and suggests bereavement as well as loneliness.

3. This sonnet, from the fourteen which Pessoa entitled 'Stations of the Cross', was written on 25 July 1914, and was published in the only number of *Centauro* to appear: October–December 1916.

5. *Boabdil*: Abū' Abd Allāh, the last Moorish king of Granada. He was defeated by Ferdinand and Isabel, the 'Catholic Kings', who took the city in 1492.

14. *dead in me*: literally 'which I died'. This is not the only occasion on which Pessoa used the verb *morrer* transitively: for other examples see Prado Coelho, *Diversidade e Unidade* etc, p. 146.

4. Written in 1914 or 1915, and published, like no. VI of the same series, in *Centauro*. Elsewhere, too, Pessoa speaks of himself as the medium of a higher power, cf. the line 'God made my shivering nerves His human lyre', in an undated English poem (ed. G. R. Lind, 'Oito poemas ingleses inéditos de Fernando Pessoa', *Ocidente* LXXIV (1968), p. 280); also no. 31 below.

1. *Sent as the envoy* . . . Álvaro de Campos, too, refers to himself as an envoy, see no. 27 below, l.29.

3–4. Cf. no. XXV of Pessoa's *35 Sonnets*: 'An unknown language speaks in us, which we / Are at the words of, fronted from reality'.

11. *the desert of self*. Elsewhere, Pessoa refers to the self as a hell (in an English poem dated 16 October 1907, publ. by Lind in *Portugiesische Forschungen* VI (1966) p. 142: 'my being's hell'), and as a prison (see below, no. 14 l.9 and no. 67 l.5).

12–13. Compare no. XXIV of the *35 Sonnets*: 'Something in me was born before the stars / And saw the sun begin from far away. . . . It dates remoter than God's birth can reach . . .'

5. Written on 14 March 1917, but not published in the poet's life-time.

6. Published in the review *Ressurreição* no. 9, February 1920.

7. Published in *Contemporânea* no. 6, December 1922. The religious scepticism expressed here goes far deeper than anything Pessoa wrote as Ricardo Reis: Reis at least displays an optimistic faith in the gods of antiquity (see in particular nos. 52 and 55), but regards Christianity as an intrusive and

gloomy religion. This poem is deeply pessimistic in suggesting that *no* religion holds or has ever held the truth.

8.   Dated 29 August 1924, and published in *Presença* nos. 31–2, March–June 1931.

30. This idea amounts to an obsession in Pessoa's poetry. For a vivid expression of it compare no. VII of the *Inscriptions*: 'Dreaming that I slept not, I slept my dream'.

44–5. *a wall/In my deserted garden*. The clue to this allusion is to be found, I think, in one of the early poems of Caeiro. In *The Keeper of Flocks* no. IV the poet says 'I felt familiar and at home,/As if I had spent my life/Quietly, *like the garden wall*'.

48–50. The poem ends with an image of astonishing originality and aptness, and the title is explained.

9.   Date of composition unknown. Published in *Contemporânea*, 3rd series, no. 1, 1926. The title means literally, 'His mother's boy', but as this term is a disparaging one in English, and 'His mother's darling' even worse, I have ventured to render it by 'His mother's very own'. The poem may have been inspired by Rimbaud's sonnet *Le dormeur du val*, or by a reminiscence of a lithograph (see above, p. 48 and note 79): the two possibilities are not mutually exclusive. Rimbaud's poem ends with the dramatic revelation, hitherto withheld, that the 'sleeper' is not asleep, but dead: 'Il a deux trous rouges au côté droit'. Pessoa tells us in the very first stanza that the young man is dead, 'pierced by two bullets'.

10.   Written on 20 August 1930.

11.   Written on 1 April 1931, and published in *Presença* no. 36, November 1932. This is perhaps Pessoa's best-known poem: it summarizes in lapidary fashion the relationship between thought, feeling, and poetic expression. The poet has feelings, but he has to intellectualize them in order to convey them to others. The reader, at the other end, does not feel what the poet originally felt, because he is not the poet. He receives only an intellectualized version, which remains at the intellectual level. That is why, in the last stanza, the heart is said to entertain the mind.

12.   Published in *Presença* no. 38, April 1933.

1–2. A striking anticipation of these lines is to be found in an English poem entitled *Woe supreme* and dated 8 June 1907. It begins 'A friend once said to me: "All that thou writest,/ Surely 'tis fancy, and pretence, and feigned..." ' (ed.

G. R. Lind, *Portugiesische Forschungen der Görresgesellschaft,* VI (1966) pp. 153–4).

13. Written on 5 September 1933.

   12. Literally 'half outline and half mist'.

14. Dated 2 October 1933. This is one of many poems in which Pessoa speaks longingly of what he once was, and regrets the irreversible nature of the past.

   8. Compare no. 12, ll.1–2.

   9. Cf. no. 4, l.11 and note; also no. 67, l.5.

15. Dated 11 June 1934. The theme of something sensed in sleep, and lost on awakening, is well illustrated here; but it occurs in several of the orthonymic poems.

   12. 'Not thinking', for this obsessively intellectual poet, seems to have represented a state of ideal happiness.

16. Dated 10 January 1922, and published in *Contemporânea* 4–6, October–December 1922: later incorporated in *Mensagem* (1934).

   9. *Cape Bojador*: a promontory on the West Coast of Africa, in Spanish Sahara, and lying slightly to the south of the Canary Islands. It was the southern limit of Portuguese exploration, until it was rounded in 1434 by the navigator Gil Eanes.

17. Dated 20 February 1933, and published in *Mensagem* in the following year. Dom Sebastian was killed in August 1578 in the tragic defeat of Alcázar Kebir in Morocco—hence the reference to the 'sandy waste' in l.4. His 'madness' was the driving ambition to make Portugal greater. According to later legends, the king did not die, and would one day come again, a belief known as *sebastianismo*. When, in 1923, an organization of Lisbon students attacked the poet Raul Leal, suggesting that he was mad, Pessoa defended him and wrote, in his pamphlet *Concerning a student manifesto*: 'It often happens that what strikes us as madness in others is nothing but our own inability to understand them. . . . Heroes are mad, saints are mad, geniuses are mad, and without them mankind is a mere animal species, just so many *postponed and procreating corpses*' (my italics). Ten years later, he linked this idea with the historical figure of Dom Sebastian.

18. Dated 26 March 1934, and published in *Mensagem* in December of the same year.

   6–10. This stanza is an anacoluthon in the original: the if-clause is followed, first by a dependent noun clause, and then by a relative clause. There is no main clause at all. I have taken the liberty of turning the dependent noun clause into a main clause.

13. The 'King who waits' is of course Dom Sebastian, and the hope of which he speaks is that of the Nation. The Islands of the Blest, known to the Romans as *Fortunatae Insulae*, were believed to lie somewhere to the west, and are usually identified with the Canary Islands. It is not without interest that in the twelfth century Geoffrey of Monmouth gave the name *Insula Fortunata*, as well as *Avalon*, to the island to which King Arthur was conveyed to be healed of his wounds (See Geoffrey's *Vita Merlini*, ed. Faral, ll.908–31). Arthur, like Dom Sebastian, was expected to return one day.

ÁLVARO DE CAMPOS

19.   Dated 30 June 1914. Though one of the finest poems Pessoa ever wrote, it was published only after his death, in the *Revista de Portugal* no. 4, July 1938. It is the longer of two poems which he entitled *Two excerpts from Odes*, with the parenthetical addition 'Endings of two odes, of course'. We have seen (Introduction, pp. 14–15) that Pessoa gave the name *Odes* to some of the early Campos poems. This one takes the form of a sustained apostrophe to Night. There is an apostrophe to Night, strikingly similar in tone, in the long poem *Passagem das Horas* which 'Campos' wrote nearly two years later, but it is much shorter, being merely incidental. A few lines will give some idea of the similarity (*Poesias* pp. 218–20): 'Come, oh Night . . . come and drown me in you./ Oh tenderness from Beyond, lady of infinite grief./Outward sorrow of the Earth, silent weeping of the World./ Gentle age-old hand of feelings without gesture,/Elder sister, virgin and sad, of unrelated ideas,/Bride forever awaiting our unfulfilled intentions—/The ever-abandoned direction of our destiny,/Our joyless heathen uncertainty/ Our faithless Christian weakness,/Our limp Buddhism. . . . Be to me a mother, silent Night/You who take the world from the world, who are peace,/You who do not exist, who are but the absence of light. . . . Come to me, oh Night, stretch out your hands to me,/And be coolness and relief, oh Night, upon my brow/You whose coming is so gentle that it

seems a going hence . . .'.

45–6. *Mater-Dolorosa*. . . . *Turris-Eburnea*: The first is from the medieval hymn, *Stabat Mater*, attributed to Jacopone da Todi († 1306): the second, as applied to the Virgin, is from the Litany, but comes eventually from the Song of Songs. The adjectives *dolorosa* and *eburnea* could be Portuguese as well as Latin, and have the same meaning in the one language as in the other. It thus follows that the phrases are less 'opaque' for Portuguese readers than for English ones. Even so, they are best left untranslated: for one thing 'ivory tower' has (thanks, it seems, to Sainte-Beuve) acquired in English quite different connotations, which would be incongruous here. The religious associations continue the reference to Night as 'Our Lady' in l.20.

71–2. The incomplete relatives of the original have a somewhat exclamatory effect.

76. *mares maiores* 'wider seas': this phrase is also in *Ode Marítima*.

91. *Como* . . . ('like'). I adopt the reading of *Revista de Portugal* here. The Ática edition has *com* 'with', which makes good sense but spoils the parallel with l.90.

20. Published in *Contemporânea* no. 8, 1923.

4. Cf. Campos, *Poesias* p. 114 where, referring to the 'sudden horror of a funeral procession', the poet adds: 'There goes the conclusion'.

12. *guardem-a*: strict grammar calls for *guardem-na*.

13. Campos is indeed a technician—an engineer.

17. *quotidiano*. In the poem *Passagem das Horas* too (dated May 1916), Campos speaks of the difficulty he has in coming to terms with life, and claims he is unable to be 'everyday' (pp. 218–19).

35. *the Abyss and Silence:* i.e. Death.

21. Dated 26 April 1926, and published in *Contemporânea*, 3rd series, no. 2, June 1926.

9. *da rua*. I adopt here the reading of *Contemporânea*, which seems to me the correct one. The Ática edn. has *na rua* 'in the street'.

13. Cf. 'Ev'n as I dream it, it is not', a line occurring in an English poem written in 1915 or 1916: see G.R.Lind, *Ocidente*, LXXIV (1968) p. 268.

18. *drifting*. Literally 'rudderless'.

32. For the notion of 'lost childhood', see also Campos, *Poesias* p. 53, *Esta velha angústia*, dated 16 June 1934.

39. Cf. no. I of the *35 Sonnets*, ll.13–14: 'We are our dreams of ourselves, souls by gleams,/And each to each other dreams of others' dreams'.

43. *A pointless passer-by*. Cf. the prose *Livro do Desassossêgo*, by 'Bernardo Soares', another heteronym: 'Passing everything by, even my own soul' (ed. in extract as *Páginas escolhidas*, by Petrus, p. 43).

48. The 'doom-laden castle of having to live' is not far from the image of the prison or dungeon which Pessoa uses in other poems, e.g. nos. 14 and 67.

56–8. *The magic mirror shattered*, etc. A poignant reference to the fragmentation of personality which Pessoa's work reflects. Cf. Campos, *Passagem das Horas*, p. 221 *Multipliquei-me para me sentir*: 'I became many so as to feel myself'.

22. Dated 26 April 1926. A strikingly original treatment of the theme of suicide, in which the arguments for (rather than against) taking one's life are ruthlessly enumerated. It is to be noted that this poem was written on the tenth anniversary of the suicide of Pessoa's closest friend, Mário de Sá-Carneiro.

33. *telling funny stories in their heartbreak*: a by no means unheard-of occurrence at wakes in Portugal.

35. *all those sobs and tears*. The word *carpidação* appears to be of Pessoa's own devising. The basis for it is the verb *carpir*, 'to lament' 'to grieve', and it is clearly meant to have a pejorative and unsympathetic flavour.

64. *objective subjectivity*: because we are the show and the spectators at the same time.

70. *do you . . . love life with all your fat* ? Literally, 'do you love life obesely ?'

23. Written on 15 January 1928, and published in *Presença* no. 39, July 1933. A remarkable statement of the conflict in the poet's mind between reality and dream, between superficial evidence and metaphysical doubt. The tobacco-shop in question has been tentatively identified with the 'Havanera dos Retroseiros', formerly on the corner of the Rua dos Retroseiros and the Rua da Prata, and thus opposite one of the offices where Pessoa worked (see Luís Pedro Moitinho de Almeida, *Algumas notas biográficas sobre Fernando Pessoa*, Setubal, 1954, pp. 8–9).

17–18. The image of a train, incidental here, becomes the main theme of the poem *Là-bas, je ne sais où*, also by Campos (*Poesias*, pp. 305–7).

25. Cf. 'I that have failed in everything', in the last of the *35 Sonnets*.

41–2. *Every asylum* etc. In an ms. note (tentatively dated 1915), Pessoa concludes that no sane person can be certain of anything: certainty is to be found only in lunatic asylums. See *Textos filosóficos* II. p. 246–7.

52. Cf. the line 'Dreaming, I conquered worlds', in the *Faust* fragment (*Poemas dramáticos*, p. 99).

72 ff. At this point the poet apostrophizes a child he can see eating sweets in the street outside, an irritating reminder of reality.

87 ff. An ironical variation on the stock classical invocation of a Muse.

88. *conceived as a statue, but alive*: one of many expressions of an impossible ideal. Pessoa used this idea again in an orthonymic poem entitled *O último sortilégio*, which he wrote on 15 October 1930 and published in *Presença* no. 29 in December of the same year: 'Let the last of my spells/Turn me into a living statue of myself'.

96–7. *I invoke/Myself and find nothing there*. Cf. no. 32, ll.1–5.

105. In another poem, dated 16 June 1934, Campos, speaking of the house opposite, says: 'There are people I don't know living there. . . . Happy because they are not me' (*Poesias*, p. 55). In an English poem written in October 1916, Pessoa had already written of 'homes happy because not his' (*Ocidente*, LXXIV (1968) p. 287).

141–5. Here Campos begins to realize that his speculations are getting him nowhere: he has merely come round to his starting-point again, for these lines refer back to ll.8–24.

24. Dated 12 April 1928.

Demogorgon: The authenticity of the word, and of the deity thus designated, has been in dispute since the sixteenth century. Most modern mentions of Demogorgon are traceable to Boccaccio's *Genealogie deorum gentilium libri* (see edn. of Vincenzo Romano, Bari 1951, Vol. I, pp. 12–15). It seems that Boccaccio found Demogorgon in the now lost work of an obscure mythographer named Theodontius, who in his turn derived his notion of Demogorgon from the

fifth-century commentary of Lactantius Placidus on the
Thebaid of Statius (IV, 516). The 'name' is in fact simply a mis-
reading of *demiurgon* = 'maker', in other words 'a scribal error
become god' (See Maurice Castelain, 'Demogorgon ou le
barbarisme déifié', *Bulletin de l'association Guillaume Budé*,
no. 36, July 1932, pp. 22–39; J.J. Seznec, *La survivance des
dieux antiques*, London, Warburg Institute, 1940, p. 189 and
notes; and cf. C.S. Lewis, *The discarded image*, Cambridge
University Press, 1964, pp. 39–40 'perhaps the only time a
scribal blunder underwent an apotheosis'). Scribal error or
not, Demogorgon has ever since the Renaissance been taken
seriously by poets as a mysterious and powerful deity, though
many of the references to him are purely incidental, and go
no further than Milton's allusion does in *Paradise Lost*, ii, 959ff.
Shelley, however, makes Demogorgon play an important part
in his *Prometheus Unbound*, and attributes to him a knowledge
of the future, and the power to explain human destiny.
Shelley was one of Pessoa's favourite English poets, and it is
clearly Shelley's conception of Demogorgon which Pessoa is
following in the present poem. The poet senses the presence,
or imminence, of a Power which threatens to reveal Ultimate
Truth, a prospect which he dreads, and which he appears to
identify with Death itself. Pessoa referred to Demogorgon
once again, in his *Faust* fragment, as a symbol of the horror of
the Mystery, and, more conventionally, as a name which is
fatal (See *Poemas dramáticos*, p. 95).

4–8. Horror at the prospect of revelation of the Mystery is
already vividly though naïvely expressed in two English
poems written when Pessoa was nineteen: *The Curtain*, and
Horror, quoted by G.R. Lind in *Portugiesische Forschungen der
Görresgesellschaft*, VI (1966) pp. 149–50.

11–12. *the distance from soul to soul*. In the first of the *35
Sonnets*, Pessoa speaks of 'the abyss from soul to soul'.

16. *I will not open them from life* (literally 'from living'). The
poet identifies his state of ignorance with life itself: know-
ledge would mean death.

25.   Dated 11 May 1928.

34–6. There are many similar regrets, in Pessoa's poetry, for
what never was, or for what he failed to do, or for what he
had no chance of becoming. Cf. Campos, *Poesias*, p. 113
'What I'd like to be and will never be, destroys me in the

streets'; and Pessoa, *Poesias* p. 226 'How it smiled upon me/ That which I never saw'.

39. *dreams undreamt*. Compare an English poem written in 1915 or 1916, and entitled *Suspense*: 'My undreamed dreams, pale elves,/Are now part of my flesh' (ed. Lind, *Ocidente*, LXXIV (1968) p. 270).

26. This poem was written on 13 June 1930—Pessoa's own birthday. It was published in *Presença* no. 27, June–July 1930, where it bears the date 15 October. The explanation for this apparent discrepancy is that 15 October is *Campos*'s birthday, as Pessoa indicated in his biographical notes for Campos (see above, p. 25), and as he also reminded João Gaspar Simões in a letter about this poem, dated 4 July 1930.

27. *A physical longing in my soul*. A line in the early poem *Paùis* (29.3.1913) reads 'a fleshly chill pervades my soul'.

27. Dated 6 August 1931.

14. *something better than myself*: cf. no. 31, l.7.

24. *no gardens of Proserpina*. An allusion to Swinburne's poem *The Garden of Proserpine*; i.e. a profound peace that is *not*, as in Swinburne's poem, the peace of death.

25. Pessoa vividly turns round the conventional idea of some-one pressing his face against the window: he makes life itself look in, and this is not surprising in a poet who often regards life as active, and human beings as passive, 'lived by life'. Cf. no. 59, ll.4–5 and note.

26. *rain can be seen audibly falling*. There are other examples in Pessoa's poetry of this fusion of hearing and seeing, e.g. 'And the windows of the church *seen* from outside *are the sound* of the rain *heard* from inside' (*Chuva oblíqua*, p. 28 in *Obras completas* I). Compare also '*heard* no more than what I *saw*' in no. 32 below.

29. *The envoy....* Cf. above, no. 4.

28. Dated 15 December 1932. This poem expresses a preoccupa-tion which is found elsewhere in Pessoa's work: the wish to recapture one's former self, to relive or reconstruct one's inner past. Cf. the orthonymic poem *Hoje que a tarde é calma e o céu tranquilo* 'I know not who I was in what I am today' (*Poesias* pp. 138–9), and the ode by Ricardo Reis *Se recordo quem fui, outrem me vejo*, no. 63 below.

29. Dated 9 October 1934.

28–30. The poet playfully repeats the superlative ending

alone, for emphasis. 'Superlative tiredness, -erlative, -erlative, -erlative tiredness' would convey the rhythm of the original, but it would miss the point of the adjective *supremo*, which means 'the last' as well as 'supreme'.

30.   Dated 18 December 1934.

2. . . . *they tell me everything's a symbol.* An English poem dating from not later than Autumn 1907 bears the title *All things are symbols* (listed by Lind in *Portugiesische Forschungen* . . . VI (1966) p. 132). Compare also 'All is symbol and analogy' in the *Faust* fragment (*Obras completas* VI, p. 76).

27. 'Get her young man back' is, I admit, ambiguous where the original is not: it could imply active steps on the dressmaker's part. There is no suggestion of this in the original, which says 'I would like the young man to go back to the dressmaker'.

31.   Dated 18 December 1934. For the theme, compare the thirteenth sonnet of *Stations of the Cross* (no. 4 above).

9. *writes—and means.* Literally 'writes in earnest' 'genuinely writes'.

32.   Dated 3 January 1935.

6–7. *peered / Into the well.* Literally 'leaned over'. A similar idea is expressed in the *Faust* fragment (*Poemas dramáticos*, p. 83) *Paro á beira de mim e me debruço* 'I stop at the edge of myself and peer in'. We may compare also José Régio's use of this image in his sonnet *Narciso: dobrado em dois sôbre o meu próprio poço* 'bent double over the well of myself' (publ. in 1925 in *Poemas de Deus e do diabo*).

8. *plaintively cried.* Pessoa uses the verb *balir*, normally used of the bleating of sheep. It is certainly meant to be disparaging, and thus to emphasize the uselessness of the activity.

9. Cf. no. 27, l.26 and note.

10. *dark brightness.* One of Pessoa's many oxymorons. For other examples see Prado Coelho, *Diversidade e Unidade* . . . 2nd edn. p. 156.

14. *if not, whose could it be?* A rhetorical question gets over the difficulty of rendering the original causal construction. 'Because it cannot be someone else's' is heavily prosaic.

ALBERTO CAEIRO

33.   Written in March 1914 (?)

9. *o levantar-se o vento.* This type of substantivization of the

infinitive is very typical of Pessoa. For other examples see Prado Coelho, *Diversidade e Unidade*, p. 149.

34. Written in March 1914(?) This is one of the four poems of 'The Keeper of Flocks' which Caeiro claimed were untypical, because he was ill when he wrote them. This poem is untypical because it expresses the wish to be something else, and a regret at having to hope—hardly the sentiments of a *healthy* Caeiro! The theme recurs, and is indeed given a further development, in no. XVIII, which begins with the line 'How I wish I could be the dust on the road'.

35. Published in *Athena* no. 4, January 1925.

36. Dated 13 March 1914, and published in *Athena* no. 4, January 1925.

   3. *translùcidamente*. There is a deliberate play on words here, which, fortunately, 'transparently' can convey in English.

37. Dated 11 March 1914, and published in *Athena* no. 4, January 1925.

   14-17. Caeiro is here admitting that his attitude is a difficult one to sustain, but he blames others for this.

38. Written in 1914 or 1915. The poet confesses that he has to make concessions to 'men fond of lies': he has to interpret Nature to man, and in order to do so, he has to some extent to adopt the misleading imagery of men.

39. Written in 1914, and published in *Athena* no. 4, January 1925. This poem should be taken in conjunction with no. 44 below, although the latter belongs to the 'Sporadic Poems' and not to 'The Keeper of Flocks'. The indifference of Caeiro to social reform is clearly brought out in both poems, which describe an encounter with a would-be social reformer.

   7. Literally 'the rich, who have backs just for that' i.e. backs to bear the burden of their own wealth—plus that of other people's misfortunes, which, as La Rochefoucauld observed, we are all strong enough to bear. The line is of course ironical.

   15. This line sums up Caeiro's somewhat unhelpful attitude.

   17. Caeiro's attitude towards good and evil is very like the attitude which Pessoa attributed to his prose heteronym Bernardo Soares, author of *O Livro do Desassossêgo*: 'my morality is quite simple: do neither evil nor good'. See F. E. G. Quintanilha, 'Fernando Pessoa e o *Livro do Desassossêgo*', *Ocidente* LXXV (1968) p. 137.

   20-7. What Caeiro wonders, in other words, is the *opposite* of

what a day-dreamer would have wondered. As Octavio Paz
has pointed out (*Cuadrívio* p. 147), Caeiro does not, as a rule,
relate things to each other or compare them with each other,
because each thing has so strong an individuality that no com-
parison is valid. He does, however, compare himself to a
'blind man on his mettle' in no. 43 (see below)!

32. *Só com florir*. Ática has *Só com o florir*. I adopt the reading
of *Athena*, also adopted in the Aguilar edition.

40. Written in 1914(?). Here, Caeiro endeavours not to think
about things, ask questions, or speculate. Even so, this poem
reveals that he needs all his self-control in order not to act as
more ordinary mortals do.

41. Written in 1914(?), and published in *Athena* no. 4, January
1925.

1–3. The attitude expressed in this poem is in complete con-
trast with Campos's attitude as expressed in *Demogorgon* (no.
24 above). For Caeiro, there is no mystery, and consequently
no cause for terror or agonized speculation.

4. *Que sabe o rio disso*. The Ática edition omits *disso*, but the
sense calls for it, and it is indeed present in the text as printed
in *Athena*.

42. Dated 7 May 1914.

2. In an English poem entitled *Insomnia*, written in January
1906, Pessoa speaks, this time impatiently, of 'the clock, with
its curst possession/Of night with its monotone' (See Lind,
Portugiesische Forschungen . . . VI (1966), p. 157).

43. Written on 10 May 1914, and published in *Athena* no. 4,
January 1925.

17–22. A vivid statement of the quest for one's true self, buried
under the layers of artificiality which education and life in
society have added. Caeiro is here expressing himself in terms
strikingly reminiscent of Gide's immoralist. See *L'Immoraliste*
(1902), ed. Mercure de France, in particular pp. 82–3 and 85.
28. *on his mettle*. Literally 'stubborn': he thinks he knows the
way, and will not accept help.

34–41. It is rare for Caeiro to *describe* a natural phenomenon.
37–9. *E que o sol . . . Ainda assim já se lhe vêem*. A *reprise* con-
struction. It looks at first as if *o sol* is going to be the subject of
a verb: instead, it becomes in l.39 an indirect object.

44. Published in *Athena* no. 5, February 1925. It is not known
whether it was written soon after no. 39, of which it is a

sequel, or whether it was first written only after that poem had already been published, i.e. in the previous number of *Athena*.

45. Written on 7 November 1915, and published in *Athena* no. 5, February 1925.

14. *my brother.* 'My sister' in the original, but stones are feminine in Portuguese. It is interesting to note that in one of the four poems which Caeiro wrote when he was ill, he so far forgot himself as to call plants his brothers (no. XVII of 'The Keeper of Flocks'). Álvaro de Campos, for his part, is not ashamed to call trees his brothers; indeed, he confesses that he feels a closer affinity with them than with workmen: see *Passagem das Horas* (p. 226 of *Poesias*).

29. Cf. no. XV of the *35 Sonnets*, ll.6–7, and no. 31 above.

46. Dated 7 November 1915, and published in *Athena* no. 5, February 1925.

15. In Pessoa's copy of Whitman's *Leaves of Grass*, the line 'What will be will be well, for what is is well' is underlined.

19. Note the elaborate internal rhyme in the original.

47. Dated 7 November 1915, and published in *Athena* no. 5, February 1925.

7–12. These somewhat cryptic lines could be related to the view Pessoa expressed in an English essay on the posthumous fame of literary works, entitled *Erostratus* (possibly to be dated 1925): 'Nothing worth expressing ever remains unexpressed; it is against the nature of things that it should remain so'. He goes on to say that merely by existing, a work of art expresses something. See *Páginas de estética e de teoria e crítica literárias*, ed. G. R. Lind & J. do Prado Coelho, p. 208.

33–5. Yet, in another of the 'Sporadic Poems' (*Poemas* p. 87), Caeiro claims that he sees things (e.g. rivers, clouds etc) *better* when accompanied by his beloved. There is an element of contradiction here, but at least his preoccupation, whether he is in love or not, is with looking at 'things which simply exist'.

48. Dated 8 November 1915.

49. Dated 19 July 1920.

14–18. Caeiro's ideal is the opposite of that of, for example, a symbolist poet like Mallarmé, for Caeiro is exclusively concerned with real objects, and not with their ideal quintessence. He is *not* attempting to convey a supernatural experience in the language of visible things.

RICARDO REIS

50. Dated 12 June 1914.

29. *the gloomy boatman.* I.e. Charon, the boatman who, in the Underworld, ferried the souls of the dead across the Styx.

51. Dated 30 July 1914.

7. *Just so.* Literally 'not otherwise'—a deliberate imitation of the Latin litotes *non aliter* or *haud secus.* In English, however, 'not otherwise' savours of conditions, and tends to mean 'only on this condition', and this would lead the reader far from the point which is being made.

7–8. Pessoa expresses elsewhere too the conviction (which he regards as essentially pagan) that the gods, as much as men, are in the grip of Fate. See *Textos filosóficos* II, pp. 92–4.

52. Dated 9 August 1914. A vivid statement of Reis's anti-Christian sentiments. His objection to Christianity is that it is vague, and not immediate, i.e. not manifest in his surroundings, whereas, he claims, the pagan gods are specifically manifest in all natural phenomena. Christianity, for Reis, is too exclusively concerned with the hereafter (but see also no. 55).

25. *procos. Proco* is not really a Portuguese word at all: Pessoa has simply coined it for the occasion, from Latin *procus* 'wooer', 'suitor'.

53. Dated 1 June 1916.

7–8. As foreshadowed in ll.1 and 3, the poet dissociates himself from national or international affairs. When this poem was written, Portugal had been at war with Austria and Germany for three months. Reis does not normally refer to current affairs at all, and even here it is to be noted that he mentions them only in order to deny that he has any interest in them.

54. Dated 1 July 1916.

16–17. Cf. Caeiro in no. XXIII of 'The Keeper of Flocks': 'My gaze . . . asks no questions'.

25. *Porque não se pensam.* In a note possibly to be dated 1915, Pessoa states that in most metaphysical systems the gods *do* 'think themselves'—that is, think themselves into being. See *Textos filosóficos* II, p. 225.

55. Dated 11–12 September 1916. This poem is in some sort complementary to no. 52, and a further reason is found for rejecting Christianity—it does not even offer a worth-while after-life. The Christian has nothing to look forward to after

death, unless the *pagan* gods take pity on him and forgive him for his neglect of them.

1. *Happy is he* etc. A classical echo, possibly inspired by the beginning of Horace's second Epode: *Beatus ille,* (*qui procul negotiis*). Reis begins another ode in the same way: *Felizes, cujos corpos sob as árvores* (*Odes*, p. 57).

5. Note the chiasmus in this line.

19–20. The obol, or small coin which had to be paid to Charon the ferryman (see note to no. 50 above) was placed in the dead man's mouth.

56. Dated 22 October 1923, and published in *Athena* no. 1, October 1924.

4. *Nothing twice over*. Literally 'nothing inside nothing'— nothing, with another layer of nothing inside it.

6. *As Parcas três*. I.e. the three goddesses of Fate, the Parcae: Clotho, Lachesis and Atropos to the Greeks.

57. Written on 17 November 1923, and published in *Athena* no. 1, October 1924.

6. Yet another reference to Charon's ferry.

58. Dated 19 November 1927.

5. *refusemos*. A deliberate archaism: the verb *refusar* has not been in current use since the sixteenth century, having been generally replaced by *recusar*.

9–11. I cannot do justice to the highly inverted word-order of the original.

59. Dated 20 February 1928. One of the finest of the *Odes*.

3. *The revellers laugh*. Literally 'It is carnival-time and they are laughing'—but *entrudo* can also mean revelry in general, and I therefore simplify for the sake of brevity.

4–5. Cf. no. XII of the English *Inscriptions* 'Life lived us, not we life'.

10. Literally 'With roses, though with false ones, let them weave . . .'

60. Written on 7 June 1928.

5–6. Cf. the orthonymic poem *Hoje que a tarde é calma . . .* (*Poesias* pp. 138–9) 'I look at all my past and see / I was what was around me'. Note also a line in Whitman's *There was a child went forth*: 'And the first object he look'd upon, that object he became', and cf. Tennyson, *Ulysses* l.18: 'I am a part of all that I have met'...

8. *O que vi . . .* The Ática edition has *Do que vi*. I adopt the

emendation proposed by Jacinto do Prado Coelho in *A bem da língua portuguesa. Boletim mensal da sociedade de língua portuguesa* III (1952), pp. 275-7.

61.   Dated 20 November 1928.

1. Once again I am obliged to conventionalize the word-order. Literally, this line reads 'Not even the humble grass if Fate forgets'. This goes far beyond the normal poetic inversions of Portuguese.

5-6. For this theme, see also no. 28 and note, and no. 63 below.

62.   Dated 20 November 1928. One of the most lapidary of the *Odes*.

5-6. Pessoa is here taking advantage of the twofold function of the verb *dever* in Portuguese: 'to owe' and 'to have to'. Literally: 'we owe nothing to fate, except having to have one'—i.e a fate.

63.   Dated 26 May 1930. For the theme, see no. 61 above, and note to no. 28.

10. *My memory*—in the sense of 'the memory of me' 'what I remember of myself'.

64.   Dated 1 November 1930.

7. *Quem quer pouco, tem tudo*. This notion is the corollary of Horace's *Multa petentibus / Desunt multa* 'He who seeks much, gets little' (*Odes*, III, xvi, 42-3).

9. *Homem*: an apposition used adversatively. The sense is, of course, '*though* a man': a Latinism.

65.   Dated 12 November 1930.

3. The pronoun *o* stands for the adjective *jovem*, which is introduced only in the next line—a highly artificial word-order.

66.   Dated 14 March 1931. The starting-point for this ode is once more the Horatian *Multa petentibus / Desunt multa* (see no. 64). Precisely because he is convinced by Horace's formula, the poet limits his desires and gratefully accepts what comes his way.

11-12. *o dado . . . o tido*: participles used as substantives.

67.   Dated 19 November 1933.

5. Cf. no. 4, l.11. and note; and no. 14, l.9.

9. A strongly alliterative line.

10. Reis's comment on infinity recalls a remark attributed to Caeiro by Álvaro de Campos: 'They say space is infinite.

Where did they see that in space ?' (*Páginas de doutrina estética*, p. 208).

11–12. A relative of Ricardo Reis is made to summarize Reis's attitude on this point in a manuscript note possibly to be dated 1915: 'We must try to give ourselves the illusion of calm, of freedom and happiness, unattainable things, because as for freedom, the gods themselves—burdened by Fate—do not possess it' (*Páginas íntimas* pp. 386–7).

68.   Not dated. Reis contrasts the clear-sighted pagan attitude with the vagueness of the Christian view of the world. *O vago* and *misteriosamente* in ll.5–6 are connected with the *veils* referred to in ll.15–16. As in no. 55, the Christian is regarded as offensive to the gods.

69.   Not dated. This ode is a plea for an impossible aloofness from all human emotion, for a state of complete freedom from any kind of involvement with one's environment.

70.   Not dated. This time, Reis has some reservations about the nature of the gods, and advocates a somewhat non-committal attitude.

1–3. A *reprise* construction. *Gesto* is 'taken up' in l.3 by means of the pronoun *lo*.

BIBLIOGRAPHY

1. Editions of the poetic works.
(i) *Obras completas de Fernando Pessoa*, ed. João Gaspar Simões and Luís de Montalvor. Lisbon: Edições Ática, 1942–56, in eight volumes as follows:
1 Poesias de Fernando Pessoa
2 Poesias de Álvaro de Campos
3 Poemas de Alberto Caeiro
4 Odes de Ricardo Reis
5 Mensagem, por Fernando Pessoa
6 Poemas dramáticos de Fernando Pessoa
7 Poesias inéditas (1930–5) de Fernando Pessoa
8 Poesias inéditas (1919–30) de Fernando Pessoa
(ii) Fernando Pessoa, *Obra poética*, ed. Maria Aliete Galhoz. Rio de Janeiro: Aguilar, 1960; 2nd edition 1965. This edition has a valuable introduction, and includes the English poems published in the poet's lifetime.

2. Editions of the prose writings.

Cartas de Fernando Pessoa a Armando Cortes-Rodrigues, ed.
Joel Serrão. Lisbon: Confluência, 1945.

Páginas de doutrina estética, ed. Jorge de Sena. Lisbon:
Inquérito, 1946.

Cartas de Fernando Pessoa a João Gaspar Simões, ed. João
Gaspar Simões. Lisbon: Europa América, 1957.

Páginas íntimas e de auto-interpretação, ed. Jacinto do Prado
Coelho and Georg Rudolf Lind. Lisbon: Ática, 1966.

Páginas de estética e de teoria e crítica literárias, ed. Georg Rudolf
Lind and Jacinto do Prado Coelho. Lisbon: Ática, 1966.

Textos filosóficos, ed. António de Pina Coelho. Lisbon:
Ática, 1968, 2 vols.

3. Critical studies
(a) in Portuguese

João Gaspar Simões, *Vida e obra de Fernando Pessoa. História
duma geração*, 2 vols., Lisbon: Livraria Bertrand, 1950.
Indispensable though marred by Freudian *Tendenz* and by
many errors of fact, particularly in biographical details.

Eduardo Freitas da Costa, *Fernando Pessoa—Notas a uma
biografia romanceada*. Lisbon: Guimarães & Cia, editores,
1951. Contains important correctives to the above.

Jacinto do Prado Coelho, *Diversidade e Unidade em Fernando
Pessoa*. Lisbon: Editorial Verbo, 2nd edn., revised and
augmented, 1963. By far the best critical study, it goes
a long way towards reconciling apparent contradictions.

Adolfo Casais Monteiro, *Fernando Pessoa e a crítica*. Lisbon:
Inquérito, 1952. A valuable survey of critical studies
published up to 1952.

Adolfo Casais Monteiro, *Fernando Pessoa, o insincero verídico*.
Lisbon: Inquérito, 1954. Deals with the vexed question of
Pessoa's sincerity.

Maria da Encarnação Monteiro, *Incidências inglesas na poesia
de Fernando Pessoa*. Coimbra, 1956. Studies the English
poems and the influence of English literature on the poet.

Mário Sacramento, *Fernando Pessoa, poeta da hora absurda*.
Lisbon: Contraponto, 1959. A useful assessment of
Pessoa's originality and of the unity of his work.

António Quadros, *Fernando Pessoa. A obra e o homem*.
Lisbon: Editora Arcádia, 1960.

A concise and useful study of the life and works.

Georg Rudolf Lind, *Teoria poética de Fernando Pessoa*. Oporto: Editorial Inova, 1970. Systematically reconstructs Pessoa's poetic theory from his recently published prose writings, and relates it to his poetic practice.

(b) in French

Pierre Hourcade, 'À propos de Fernando Pessoa', *Bulletin des études portugaises*, nlle. série, xv (1951) pp. 151–80. A searching review-article on the studies of Pessoa by Gaspar Simões and Prado Coelho (1st edn.), with many original observations.

Armand Guibert, *Fernando Pessoa*, 'Poètes d'aujourd'hui' no. 73) Paris: Seghers, 1960. A useful study, published with French translations of several poems.

Jacques Borel, 'Fernando Pessoa ou le poète pulvérisé', *Critique*, (décembre 1962) pp. 1040–55.

Alain Bosquet, 'Fernando Pessoa ou les délices du doute', a chapter (pp. 174–85), in Bosquet's *Verbe et Vertige—situations de la poésie*. Paris: Hachette, 1961.

Maria Aliete Galhoz has publ. in *Bulletin des études portugaises*, nlle. série XXIII (1961) a French translation of her introduction to the 1960 (Aguilar) edition of Pessoa's poetic works.

(c) in English

J. M. Parker, in *Three twentieth-century Portuguese poets*. Johannesburg: Witwatersrand University Press, 1960 (includes literal translations of nine poems).

Hubert Jennings, *The Durban High School Story 1866–1966*, pp. 99–110. Durban, Natal: Brown, Davis & Platt Ltd., 1966.

Américo da Costa Ramalho, 'Fernando Pessoa' in *Portuguese Essays*. Lisbon: Secretariado Nacional da Informação, 1963 (includes a few translations by Joseph Luke Agneta and Jean Longland).

Édouard Roditi, 'The several names of Fernando Pessoa', *Poetry* (Chicago) 87 (Oct. 1955) pp. 40–4. The same volume contains (pp. 26–9) translations, also by Roditi, of a few of Pessoa's poems.

Roy Campbell, *Portugal*, pp. 156–60. London: Max Reinhardt, 1957 (very brief notes on the poet, and translations of four poems).

List of Poems

FERNANDO PESSOA